spark*

spark*

—

A DIALOGUE ABOUT CREATIVITY AND GOD'S BURNING DESIRE
TO LIGHT THE WORLD THROUGH THE HUMAN HEART

—

—

TRAVIS WRIGHT

—

MIRꓤOR

Unless otherwise noted, all biblical quotations are taken from the Zondervan NIV Study Bible (Fully Revised), copyright © 1985, 1995, 2002 by The Zondervan Corporation.

Published in San Francisco, California, by Mirror Press.

Mirror Press titles may be purchased in bulk for educational, business, fund-raising, or sales promotional use. For information, please e-mail books@mirrorSF.com

Exterior and interior design my Mirror.

Printed in the United States of America

ISBN-13: 978-0615672977 (Mirror Press)
ISBN-10: 0615672973

To Jessica, my soul mate and best friend — for seeing something in me I couldn't see myself.

CONTENTS

"Your time is limited, so don't waste it living someone else's life. Don't be trapped by dogma — which is living with the results of other people's thinking. Don't let the noise of others' opinions drown out your own inner voice. And most important, have the courage to follow your heart and intuition. They somehow already know what you truly want to become. Everything else is secondary."

—Steve Jobs

PROLOGUE
INTO THE SUNRISE

"Vulnerability is the birthplace of innovation, creativity and change."

—Brené Brown

A DIALOGUE ABOUT CREATIVITY

SPARK* is a dialogue about creativity.

But this is not about creativity in the external sense of brainstorming or coming up with new ideas. It's a discussion around the internal experience of creativity and what it means to be a creator.

The fulfillment of creative inspiration is more of a reflex, a necessity, in the face of the internal friction and angst that exists within us, pressing us ever deeper into ourselves in our need to explore and expose what it is that is stirring inside us. The revelations of these urges pour themselves out through limitless mediums.

This is not about mediums either.

In our expressions of creativity there exists an experience much more profound than simply finding resolution. Creativity (and the outward acts of creation it demands) is full of fear and vulnerability. Creative resolution demands a terrifying, yet unavoidable, openness of the heart — a trust that there is purpose in the risk.

This exposing of what lies within us leaves us naked before an unforgiving world. The humility of creation is so real, so overwhelming, it often brings us to our knees.

Yet interwoven within this visceral, emotional experience of creativity is the reality of the soul that we have been created in the image of a Creator who is ever beckoning us. And the more we open ourselves to the depths of what it means to be a creator, the more we seem to find of Him — and in this intimacy, we begin to see how just as His creation speaks of His heart, our creativity does too.

It is in this place of complexity, friction, intimacy, and humility that my own heart wishes to explore creativity, and what it means to be a creator — beckoned by an inspiration, a need to create, that I still don't fully understand, carried by a restless need for change that only the death of winter and the rebirth of spring can bring, and captivated by the possibility of what lies beneath the surface of a heart eerily longing to be broken open, into the sunrise we go.

A WARNING

Before we get started, I need to warn you.

What you're about to read is quite personal.

Driven by a conviction to uproot everything I am, in these pages I've tried to capture the experience of what it means to be human, to be a creator, to be me — in all the emotions, the pain and joy, the struggles and victories, the ugliness and beauty.

What follows is a collection of journal entries and essays I've penned over the past year. Most appear in the order that I originally wrote them and were written in the moment, in the midst of the experiences and swelling of emotions that moved me to write. As a result, some of the passages have

the potential to be incredibly volatile, raw, expressive —
acute; which can happen when we put pen to paper while
we're caught up in the emotions of the present and lacking
the benefit of perspective — or reconciliation — that only
the passage of time can bring.

And that's okay.

Unlike the way I live most of my life, I've tried to eliminate
any trace of a facade from these pages. I don't want this
to be diluted. I don't want this to be polished. I don't want
every page in this book to "feel good." That's not what real
life is like. Life is messy, and so are we. As much as it scares
me, it doesn't feel right to ignore the brokenness that exists
within me — within all of us, really.

Real life only exists in the contrast.

Opening ourselves up to the world can be dangerous,
though. Exposing ourselves is full of risk, because it gives
not only our heart, but the demons inside our souls, a voice.
And in the face of that risk, I confess, I am more terrified
than I have ever felt in my life — because I don't fully know
what's lurking beneath the surface.

It's my hope that, in those times where my struggling heart
has poured itself out through its wounds, you'll hear a voice
of humility and longing — and not that of malice.

In the face of my anxieties, I'm pouring myself into these
pages because emptying myself completely, in all the
beauty and ugliness that comes along with it, feels like the
only way to get to the heart of who I am.

In our cosmetic culture it's easy to forget, to ignore, that we have wounds — and scars. On the surface we're "doing good," but if we dig deep enough, and listen close enough, we realize those wounds have voices too.

I think it's important to hear what they have to say — as the most important lessons always seem to come gift-wrapped in pain.

In seasons of brokenness, more than anything, we desperately need to know we're not alone — we need someone to tell us that, despite the present darkness, things do in fact get better.

We need hope.

Our stories of pain, struggle, loss, survival, redemption, forgiveness — our wounds and scars — are the mediums God uses to deliver hope to a dark and broken world. But in order for God to use them, we must first have the courage to embrace them.

Like most everything in life, though, things are easier said than done. I've spent most of my life wrestling with wounds I can barely define, let alone escape.

No matter how hard I try, I can't seem to shake these questions and contradictions. They are holding my soul, and my life, hostage. I desperately need to separate who I am from who I've become — but I don't know how.

The struggle has left me even more broken, empty, and lost in the mess that has become my life. So with no where else to turn, I'm throwing all these hopes and feelings, the loneliness, I can't resolve into the ether — into these pages — in hopes that even just one person might respond with, "Me, too."

As much as I'm hoping to find some shred of truth in the unraveling of myself, I have an equally intense desire to open my heart, and the wounds God has blessed me with — in hopes that even one soul may find solace and hope in knowing they are not alone, there is hope, and that no matter how far we wander astray or how broken our hearts are, our God is a lover of prodigals and a master at making all things new.

I'm living proof.

Lastly, I've called this collection of writings a "dialogue" for a reason. For me, this book is simply a few opening remarks in, what I hope will be, a lifelong conversation about our humanity, our creativity, our stories, and our Creator; a discourse where iron sharpens iron — where we learn, grow, and love God together.

These are in every sense "first" words, not "last" words.

So, I invite you.

If something in these pages stirs something in you, please join the conversation.

Call me,
Email me,
Tweet me,

Facebook me.

I'd love to hear from you.

THE POINT OF NO RETURN

I've been searching myself lately, trying to understand what it is inside me that's been burning so intensely these past few months, and why it seems to want so desperately to escape. I can only seem to catch fleeting glimpses, but its presence is always undeniable, and ever expanding in my chest. I turned to these pages in an effort to understand these urges. I hope a story worth telling emerges, but it's hard to know for sure when I don't even know where these words are coming from, or why they are coming at all.

All I know is that, for some reason, it feels like the only way to find resolution is to open myself up completely.

And the vulnerability is paralyzing.

But in the face of the fear, there's something deeper, something stronger, pulling me into the abyss — something beyond the selfish hope that something beautiful, meaningful, transcendent would escape the black box that is my soul: a longing to discover who, exactly, I am.

It seems everything I do is driven by the same gaping void. Behind every creative expression, every new medium, is a desperate prayer that I might finally find what it is that I was created for.

These pages are no different.

Despite all the soul searching I have done in my life, everywhere I've gone and everything I've done hasn't brought me any closer to the resolution for which my soul is pining. No matter where I am, the burning is still there, raging inside my chest.

It's consuming.

Years of tear- and prayer-filled nights have only begun to reveal the notion that the burning is not a desire for something that can be found "out there," but my physical body's acknowledgement of a suffocating soul that is desperately crying out for discovery, expression — rescue.

My soul is longing to be set free.

The more I try to uproot myself, the more I sense how trapped I've become by what the world has told me I need to be and what I need to believe. The noise is so deafening that it's impossible to hear the whispers I know are coming from my own heart.

If only the world had a mute button.

A blank page and some headphones is as close as I've come to finding one.

Deep down, I know our lives should be defined by who we are, not by who the world thinks we should be. But no matter how many times I tell myself this, I seem to do everything I can to forget. Call it human nature, or the demons inside me, but I seem to be hell-bent on trying to define myself through external means: money, job titles, projects, relationships, cities, trips, toys, Facebook "Likes," re-tweets, Klout scores, or whatever else I manage to project importance into. The list truly never ends.

In the emotional release that only comes from embracing the reality of complete helplessness, I think I'm finally starting to see that admitting that I don't have anything figured out might just be the first step towards figuring things out.

So with the humility that only comes from spending most of my life upside down inside myself, I'm going to let the story my heart seems so intent on telling express itself as best as I can translate. I don't really know what these pages are ultimately going to hold, but something deep within me keeps telling me to silence the fears and trust that what is coming is coming for a reason.

We are truly never more naked than when our creative heart shoves us past the point of no return.

With my heart and stomach in my throat, here we go.

ONE

ANATOMY OF A SPARK

———

"God whispers to us in our pleasures, speaks to us in our conscience, but shouts in our pains: It is His megaphone to rouse a deaf world. We are like blocks of stone...the blows of His chisel, which hurt us so much, are what make us perfect."

—*C.S. Lewis*

———

A LONG WAY FROM HOME

Once again, I found myself curled up in the bottom of the shower. My heart, my soul, my entire being, was shattered. It had been a few months since my life had exploded like a New Year's Eve fireworks show — on New Year's Eve — but I was still crashing along the rocky bottom of a life gone totally sideways. I don't know what it is, but there is something spiritual about being engulfed in falling water and swirling steam — it just seems to echo a broken soul in a way few things do.

So there I was. Broken into a million pieces. Doing my best to lose all sense of time. Hoping the heat would make me numb.

Like every clichéd story, my heart had been broken by a girl who told me she loved me but had always been in love with someone else. Our story isn't worth telling, but the sparks that flew the night everything fell apart set off a wildfire through my entire life. In a matter of seconds, my life imploded — as the pressure of all the lies finally proved too much and the truth of her transgressions gave way.

My heart had been broken many times before, but this one was different. This one literally burned me to the ground. It was as if God had tossed a match into the dry and barren field that had become my life. Nothing escaped. Maybe it's because I loved her so much. Maybe it's because the grass of my soul had become so dry, a withered and stale memory of who I used to be. In the end I'm not fully sure, but, in hindsight, there was no question God was doing a deliberate work in my life that day.

Pain is truly God's flint stone.

And though I didn't know it then, that dark day has proven to be the single most important day in my life. Not for the day's events, but for what God made from the ashes. And, despite the ugliness and pain, for it I am forever thankful.

It might seem odd to say I'm thankful for the pain, but I think most people have a hard time embracing the critical role brokenness plays in shaping who we are — who we become. Too often we turn those times of trial into resentment, unforgivingness, hate, instead of opening our eyes to the blessings they are designed to bring. Pain is a vessel, a carrier, of change. And when we refuse to accept the change, the growth, that life is offering, we become prisoners to our denial.

I feel bad for winter. It always gets a bad rap. Everyone always celebrates the spring. Yet spring would be nothing if it weren't for the death winter brings. Too often we celebrate spring itself without realizing that what we're truly celebrating is the contrast.

The key to life is the variance, as life only happens when we are able to detach ourselves from the loss of winter and embrace the promise of spring.

The beauty of time is that it brings the gift of perspective. In the years since my life imploded, I've come to see that, though the girl was the spark, she wasn't the cause. I had spent the entire twenty-two years of my life to that point crafting an identity, and ego, that proved to be as fragile as it was fake.

It was my fault.

All of it.

I don't blame her for not loving me. There really wasn't much to love back then. I was callous, arrogant, and consumed by what I thought was a promising career. I took no prisoners. Yet the irony is, I was slowly becoming a prisoner myself, a victim of my own decisions. Maybe victim isn't the right word. It implies some sort of innocence. Self-sabotage seems to be a better fit — as my broken life was nothing more than a mirror, a reflection, a culmination, of the millions of tiny decisions I'd made throughout my twenty-two years on this earth. The world, and my life, were simply reflecting the greater truth that was trapped inside my soul: I was living a life I wasn't created for.

And the scary part was, I didn't even know it.

It was impossible to comprehend in the moment how fragile and erroneous my life was because the life I was living was a life I had created.

And as precarious as my life was (and still is), all it took was the first domino to tip and instantly everything else fell with it. They always say the stock market falls faster than it rises, but believe me when I tell you, life falls infinitely faster.

Before I knew it, everything I had worked so hard to orchestrate fell apart. My relationship with the girl I thought I was going to marry imploded and I was trapped in a job and city I despised — all on the heels of four years spent practically killing myself pursing a prestigious and expensive college degree I wasn't even using (and still haven't).

I was a long, long way from home.

And the scariest part was realizing I didn't have the slightest idea where I was or how I managed to get there. Somewhere, somehow, I'd lost myself. That is to say, if I ever possessed myself at all in the first place.

How could I ever hope to return to a place, an identity, a truth, I didn't even realize I'd left behind?

Physical death by a thousand cuts.

Spiritual death by a thousand decisions.

The scariest part of spiritual death is that we become numb so slowly we don't even realize we're dying. Life truly is all in the details. Whoever coined that phrase is definitely way smarter than me. Don't let the fact that I can quote the phrase fool you. I still haven't figured it out.

That was five years ago.

And it's taken every second of those five years to even begin to rebuild my life and my belief about who I am. With five years of perspective, I can promise you the road of redemption is more difficult than you can ever imagine. God isn't simply content with restoration; God desires growth. And that means stretching us past our breaking point and interceding in the eleventh hour to carry all that we can't. But I can also promise you, beyond all doubt, the story ends well. Very well. Sitting here today, I wouldn't trade a single second of the past five years for the world. I needed every trial God sent me through.

God is truly an artist. He loves to paint stories of redemption. Stories of glory and freedom — of beauty. He breaks us because it's the only way He can bless us. But it's impossible to bless someone who refuses to accept it. And this is what we do. Every second of every day. We reject God in favor of our own version of life. In our pride, we believe our abilities, our achievements, our progress are things we've actually earned and deserve, instead of the result of His infinite generosity.

We love to give ourselves credit.

But thankfully, God loves to wash us clean.

WASH ME CLEAN

She is this city,
She's everything it's supposed to be.
These streets used to lead to something,
The lights reflecting the brilliance of her universe.
But the shades of gray cast across the sky,
Bleed out the flames as everything about her is
washed away.

But heaven's tears don't wash me clean.
The lines on my cheeks,
Drawn by the fall of lies,
Etched by the memory of innocence.

This city of angels falls,
With the feathers of her broken wings.

The fire of her lies burns everything I am.

Her words used to mean something,
They used to be light as air.
Now they're like bricks cast on top of a heart,
That doesn't have the strength to bare.

Thrown by an angel who never, ever cared.
Why don't you care?
Thrown by an angel who never, ever cared.
Why don't you, don't you?

This city of angels falls,
With the feathers of her broken wings.
The fire of her lies burns everything I am.

As the ashes that line her eyes bleed into the
night,
Love casts grace we don't deserve.
Heaven's tears come wash me clean,
Come wash me clean.

I'm so lost in this city,
I'm so lost, lost without her here.
This city feels empty,
To me it might as well be dead,
Because it only feels alive when she's here.

DEATH OF AN EGO

Not long after everything fell apart, I decided to leave my job. It was lucrative and I was on the "fast-track," but I didn't remotely love what I was doing. I was miserable. My life was already spinning. I didn't have a clue which way was up. All I knew was that I needed out.

Everything had to go.

Out of both my own desperation and God's forceful hand, the next year would ultimately erase everything I'd ever achieved and worked for. The money, the car, the house, the job, the possessions, the city, and all the God-loving friends I'd been leaning on, fell away one by one. Even my mahogany framed degree would ultimately find itself stuffed in a box under the bed in the guest bedroom of my parents' house where I would soon be living.

In every way possible, I was broken. Everything I'd ever been or ever hoped to be seemed nothing more than a fading memory. All that I had supposedly achieved in my life suddenly added up to nothing. It was as if the currency my entire life was built upon inflated like a country caught in the grip of an economic collapse. In the blink of an eye, everything I had was worthless, and everything I needed was out of reach.

An empty shell of a man and some prayers were all I had left.

I spent the first six months after leaving my job living off savings. I tried to start a business, but failed. I was out of cash and out of options, so a visit to my parents for Christmas turned into a one-way trip. I spent the next six months trying to get any kind of job I could. I think I applied to every coffee shop in a forty-five minute circle around my parents' house.

Nothing.

Finally, after months of searching, I finally managed to land a job at one of those coffee shops. In fact, the busiest coffee shop in my hometown. A town where I still knew practically everyone. I'd been gone for six years, but the faces hadn't changed much since I'd left.

Small towns have a way of staying frozen in time like that.

Day after day, I would get looks of surprise from countless people as they'd ask me why I was working there. From most it felt like pity. Others, it seemed, were awkwardly caught trying to do the math, in an attempt to understand how I, in the two years since graduating college, had come to be the one serving up their double-tall, extra-dry, low-fat cappuccino.

It didn't add up to them, and it sure as hell didn't add up to me.

I was so crippled by the shame that my stomach was in knots every day as I drove to work. The embarrassment of having to publicly showcase how badly I had somehow squandered all the opportunity I had ever been given was crippling.

I was so engulfed in failure I could vomit.

There's a line in Mat Kearney's song "Down" that really echoes close to my heart when I think of those desperate times:

> *I'm working late again, slaving to make the rent.*
> *I'm making coffee with dreams heavy as cement.*

They're coming one by one, the face of falling in love.
I write a song with a prayer as I slide the cup.

Yes, the small amount of extra money was a blessing, but this was about something far deeper than money. God put me on display because, despite all that I'd given up in my life, all that had been stripped away, there were still demons alive and well deep within my soul. Ego. Pride. Arrogance. And God wasn't going to rest until every last one of them was dead.

Humility was the only way out.

I've never heard this idea so succinctly as a co-worker of mine put it one day at that fateful coffee shop. Like me, he had achieved much in the eyes of the world. He was an incredible artist backed by a master's degree. And yet, here we were, making lattes side by side. Probably two of the most overqualified baristas you'll ever find. But aside from our education, our lives couldn't have been more different. I was beyond unhappy for reasons I couldn't pinpoint, and he seemed remarkably fulfilled and content. I couldn't come to grips with the fact that I had gone from a lucrative job to making lattes for ten dollars an hour. I was miserable and at complete odds with the work God was trying to do in my life. Yet in the midst of my own depression and, to be honest, anger, here was this guy who had seemingly "achieved" and "lost" just as much as me and was somehow truly happy. I didn't understand. So I asked him. And his reply was something that changed my life forever.

When I asked him how he was able to find joy despite the apparent struggles of our situation and the disparity of our lives when compared to our backgrounds, he simply said:

"God needs to get me low enough so he can use me."

The clarity, simplicity, and truth of his statement rocked me. And in that moment, the lights finally went on. I was miserable because my heart was after the life I was trying to create for myself and simply hoping God would play along. He was happy because his heart was after the life God was trying to *give* him. And he knew it — unequivocally. He knew who he was and what God was calling him to do. No ego. No ambition. No striving. No struggling. Only the conviction and peace that comes from fully entrusting our lives to the loving God who made us.

I finally began to understand what God was doing. He was stripping me down to the core. Grinding me down to the very essence of who I was — who He had designed me to be. Maybe this is what the Bible means when it talks about "dying to ourselves."[1]

In death we find life.

It seems that in a world full of people drowning in the idea of a success-driven life, where we must constantly edify ourselves to stay ahead; self-depreciation may be the narrowest of roads that leads to true freedom and happiness.

FACADE

Ego too weak,
To hold up the facade.
The image I've created of myself,
Shatters like the mirror I truly am.

Nothing I am,
Comes from within.
I am a mosaic,
Reflecting all my hopes contrived.

Yet reality thwarts,
Destiny scolds.
As I am forced to face,
The mirror of myself.

Reflections diverge,
From the scene,
I had hoped to paint.

Content to let the canvas burn.
The pieces of who I am,
Scatter on the floor.
Ashes drug down by the weight of truth.

TEARS OVER SMILES

Unfortunately for me, the emotional and mental pressure chamber of the coffee shop proved to be more than I could handle. God never takes us further than we can handle, and as lame as it may sound, the coffee shop was a bigger test than my heart could bare. I made it two and a half months as a barista, and was on the verge of another emotional collapse, when God graciously opened an escape hatch. And it came through something that's as much a part of me as anything else: golf.

Golf has been a huge part of my life for as long as I can remember. Though I didn't take it seriously until I reached high school, some of my fondest memories are of playing golf with my dad, uncles, and grandparents. In college, hitting golf balls on the driving range late into the night kept me sane.

I was a sophomore in high school when my grandfather Bob lost his battle with lung cancer. Six weeks later, my uncle Brad passed away from a brain aneurism while working out one night at the gym. He literally fainted in the middle of the gym and never woke up. He left behind a wife and two young children. In what seemed like an instant, they were gone.

It was the first time in my life that I had to face real tragedy, had to face the reality that our lives are truly but a flash of brilliance in the infinitely grand story God is painting. Every last moment is a gift. You blink, and they're gone. Blink again, and you're gone.

I credit my grandfather for instilling me with a love for golf and a love for craftsmanship. In my youth, we didn't always have much to talk about, but in his wood shop and on the golf course, we found a common ground for which I'm forever thankful.

My grandparents lived in Oregon much of my life. We didn't get to see them much, but I always looked forward to the trip because it meant I would be spending the afternoons with him in his wood shop or out playing golf. He was a true craftsman. He built everything from furniture to his own house. He had every tool imaginable, and he used to teach me how to use them and, together, we'd build things.

I come from a long line of homebuilders. My father has the same gift as my grandfather. He's a brilliant craftsman. And more importantly, he and my mother both possess impeccable taste and an eye for composition. An incredible house is the culmination of a million small decisions and a million more seemingly miniscule executions. And like master symphony conductors, they can unite the details better than anyone I've ever seen. Though I build things using pixels instead of lumber, those memories of learning how to design something, and build it right, are a huge part of me.

My grandfather loved three things in life: building, fishing, and golf. He made me my first set of custom golf clubs, in a time when left-handed clubs were hard to come by. I remember opening the gift Christmas morning. I remember the smile on my father's face and I remember the proud feeling of knowing my grandfather had assembled each and every one himself. When I held those clubs, I could feel the love he put into building them. I must have been seven or eight years old.

It's funny how those little moments burn themselves into our hearts like that.

My uncle Brad, my dad's younger brother, was one of the greatest men, and lovers of Jesus, I've ever known. He was my uncle, but I swear he loved me as though I was his own son. I felt like I lost a father when I lost him. I still find it hard to think of him and not smile and cry at the same time. To be honest, my tears are falling over a grin as I'm writing this. Even after all these years, it's impossible for me to hold them back.

Great people have a way of doing that to you.

Like most of us, I don't remember much of anything before the age of five. But I remember, clear as day, times when I must have only been two or three, where he would drive three hours to come visit us. My parents still tell me stories about how he'd make the trip not because he wanted to hang out with them, but because he wanted to spend time with me. I remember his black T-Top Pontiac Trans Am (the ones with the golden phoenix painted on the hood) pulling into the driveway one day with what seemed like a life-sized, neon pink, stuffed buffalo buckled into the passenger seat. His grin was so big it could have touched both horizons. I remember another time he bought me a complete San Francisco 49ers, Joe Montana football uniform. It even came with a helmet, which he somehow managed to get on sideways so he was looking out the ear hole. Thank God my parents had the presence of mind to snap a picture. It may be my favorite picture in the whole world.

During my childhood, he made countless trips from the Bay Area to our house in the foothills just to spend time with me or watch me play sports. He truly did treat me as his own son. And for his love and how much his life radiated with the love of Jesus, I am forever grateful. I still don't fully understand why he so intently spent his time and love on me, but I feel eternally indebted to him for how his investment has shaped me.

I am a better man because of him.

I'm not sure exactly why I'm telling these stories now, but it would be hard to find peace with this book if I didn't acknowledge how much those men have impacted me.

SECOND CHANCES

Until I'd graduated college, my entire working life was spent at various country clubs. I was fifteen when I got my first country club job. Too young to drive, my parents had to drive me to work. I mostly worked outside as a service attendant, helping guests and cleaning golf carts. It was an incredible opportunity as a high school kid. The tips were good and I could play as much golf as my heart desired. And I took full advantage. After about a year, a new golf club opened closer to home so I switched venues. I worked there through the rest of high school and in the summers during college. Saying golf was my life through most of high school and college may be an understatement. I was in love with the game, and still am to this day. Today though, I think I hold it so close not for the game itself, but for all the memories it has given me over the years.

A few of the golf pros I'd worked for were still at the same course when I'd moved back in with my parents. When I'd first tried to get a job after moving home, the course was one of my first stops. Unfortunately, there weren't any openings so I chose to pursue a "career" in coffee instead. When less than three months of making coffee had broken my soul and ego beyond my ability to take another second of it, I stopped back into the course to see if a spot had opened up.

By the grace of God, they gave me a job.

I was twenty-four years old and had just landed the same job I had when I was sixteen. And I was on cloud nine. When I got home, I dropped to my knees and thanked God for saving me. One more day in the coffee shop and I know my soul would have exploded.

After all I'd been through, the open door felt like a reset button. God had given me the ultimate do-over. And He placed me in exactly the same spot where my story, four years prior, had gone sideways.

Deep down, I think most of us long for second chances — there's no question that this was mine.

If I've learned anything from Jesus, it's that He loves to wipe the slate clean. So with a clean slate and an expectant heart, my mission to re-write the story of my life began.

As is the case with most auspicious stories, the beginnings are always empty of glamor and full of struggle. It was September when I started working at the golf course, which meant winter was around the corner. Before I knew it, my shifts were starting in the darkness of early morning as I, dressed in a full-blown snow jacket and gloves, scraped ice and wiped rain off golf carts. I still don't understand what possesses golfers in Northern California to endure the elements for such a dreadfully frustrating game, but I can tell you that I got to witness some of the most beautiful sunrises I've ever seen as the sun would press its way through the frozen limbs of the leafless oak trees that covered the grounds.

I think beauty is one of God's most powerful tools for the healing of a broken spirit. And through the winter, He gave it to me in heavy doses.

I ended up working at the golf course for nine months. In those months, God taught me what it means when people tell you to "bloom where you're planted." It's not easy. Though it was less public than the cafe job, I still had to face many of my parents' friends who played the course often and field the same inevitable questions about why I was the one cleaning their clubs and parking their carts.

Despite the inner struggles, my time there was exactly what I needed. The golf pros who gave me the job were beyond encouraging and supportive of the change in direction I was trying to make with my life. They knew how much I needed their help and I am forever indebted to them for their grace and generosity. In a strange way, there's something about a golf course that makes my soul feel at home. It's warm, familiar, and full of memories. And in those days, I needed a glimpse of home more than ever.

I remember the day I finally learned what it means to "bloom." The day came about eight and a half months into my tenure. I was standing in the middle of the driving range, in the middle of a torrential down pour. I had spent the last two hours digging plugged range balls out of the mud with a screw driver, one by one, and the last six months trying (unsuccessfully) to get a "real" job. I had sent out over one hundred and fifty resumes to no avail. My clothes and shoes were soaking wet and covered in mud. I couldn't feel my hands or feet. As much as I was drowning in the water, I was drowning in frustration.

I felt so defeated.

As the rain continued to pour, I looked over to my right, and there were two Hispanic maintenance workers also digging for golf balls in the bushes to the side of the driving range. They, like many, had immigrated to America for a chance at a "better life." They were facing the exact same circumstances as me, yet there was one huge difference: They were smiling. In that moment, the sound of their laughter ran me over like a bulldozer as a single thought exploded through my clouded mind:

I can't begin to imagine how much these men must have sacrificed just for the opportunity to do the work we're doing now. If they can be happy and thankful for the blessings they've been given, I can too.

In that moment, I can honestly say that for the first time in my life, I was happy exactly where I was. For the first time, I truly believed in the truth that God had me exactly where He wanted me. And I could finally grasp just how much He had provided for me, carried me, loved me — despite my blindness to it all.

I don't think I've ever had a more thankful and content heart.

Ironically enough, I landed that "real job" two weeks later. My role? Graphic Designer for a fast-growing tech start-up in my home town. Two years of crawling through the valley of my shattered life and God finally carried me to the other side.

Remember when I said that, despite our fears, despite how dark things get, the dawn always comes?

I know, because I've experienced it. More than once. And, despite the difficulty of the road God sometimes paves for us, every second, every inch, of the journey is intentional — and necessary.

The highs aren't highs without the lows.

But why would God do all this? Why is it that He's willing to go to such great lengths to save us from ourselves? To save me? We hear over and over in Sunday school how much God loves us, but hearing never really means much. As much as I can recite the fact, I know I've lived the vast majority of my life disconnected from the deep knowing that God loves me. The thought almost seems foreign because that truth is seemingly so absent from our everyday lives, from my life. I know that I don't feel Him with me every moment of the day like my beliefs tell me He is. Belief and experience can be especially far apart sometimes. For me it feels more like most of the time. I think this could be true for most of us.

So why does He love us so intently? In spite of how far we've strayed, and how much we deny and reject Him?

Because He created us.

LANTERNS

We were meticulously designed and created for a reason — with a calling that is woven into the fabric of our hearts, our souls, our desires — into our very being: *to be beacons of light to a world trapped in perpetual darkness.*

Yet despite our divinely created luminosity, the light we carry is not our own.

We are lanterns.

Our function seems simple, but lighting a lantern isn't easy. It comes at a cost. Every chemical reaction requires activation energy. We are no different. Light is the result, but light comes from something. It has a story. A beginning.

Every flame is born of a spark.

A spark is the genesis. A spark ignites. But even a spark has an anatomy, a beginning: friction.

Intense, violent, painful friction.

A spark is born from pain.

It is this friction, the pain, the grinding down of our artificial identities, the stripping away of all that we've built around ourselves, that we must endure if we truly want to know what lies beneath who we *think* we are and discover who God *knows* we are. We build ourselves and our lives up like five-year-olds with a pile of Legos. And the only way for God to put the pieces in their proper place is to pull us apart piece by piece by piece and rebuild us from the ground up.

This dismantling can be completely overwhelming. The death of my identity is the deepest pain I've ever experienced. Our humanity is at odds with the life that God wants for us. We are hell-bent on exercising our free will, our independence. We want to be known. We want to possess. We want to win.

Yet despite all this, the only thing God wants is *us*. He longs for us. He wants to see *His* creation in its full glory. And so He relentlessly pursues us. Pressing deeper and deeper into us, His love for us grinds violently against our love for ourselves. The friction is brutal, intense — painful. But sadly, most of us are numb to the pain.

We are numb because we've been dying slowly; ever trying to silence the pangs of a reality that is always beckoning us below the surface; ever trying to ignore the pain that comes from realizing the broken stories we are telling couldn't be further from the story our hearts are so desperately crying out for. The story we know we should be telling. The story we know exists but don't know how to find.

Deep down we know we are lost. Separated. Merely a shadow of what we were supposed to be. We are so disconnected from ourselves that we don't even know who we are, or where to even begin in trying to create a life worth living. So we give up. We give in. We concede. We choose to let our hearts, our desires, our passions die — suffocated slowly by the denial of their existence. We numb ourselves to the pain, the hurt, the disappointment, that swells in the wake of the identity we've lost and a life that's run away faster than we ever imagined. We hide our dreams and try everything we can to convince ourselves we "didn't want that anyway" or we're "happy with how things turned out." But the truth is, we do miss all that we've left behind. We long for second chances (even though we won't admit it). We deny the truth and save face because we know it's too late anyway. Or at least that's what we tell ourselves. Life goes on. Life goes on as our lives become echoes bouncing across the void our life was supposed to fill. We try and convince ourselves that we are happy, content, fulfilled.

But, deep down, we know we're not.

Or at least I know I'm not.

My thoughts are always consumed by the pressing feeling of the void that exists between who I am and who I should be. It hurts to accept the reality of the diminishing returns God is receiving on behalf of His investment to create me and, subsequently, chase me for the past twenty-seven years.

The hardest part is that I feel the void but don't know how I'm supposed to fill it. How can I ever hope to fully be "me," when I don't have the slightest idea who "me" is?

I know God is a huge fan of simple answers. The more I see God's love of simplicity the more I think He's a huge fan of Steven Segal movies. Four words max per sentence. No wasted syllables. No wasted effort. Exactly what's needed. Nothing more. Nothing less.

I've spent my entire life knotting up all the threads that my mind spins in its desperate search for meaning — for purpose. Meanwhile, the answer (I'm sure) is some elemental, clichéd nugget of truth that holds the entire universe in its hand. It's the galaxy hidden in the cat's collar (anyone a *Men In Black* fan?). So small and innocent most will never find it.

Hidden in plain view.

A big part of me has been consumed with this notion that if I had a better understanding of who God is, I'd have a better understanding of who I am. Call it God's guiding hand, or just another desperate guess, but on a prayer, I'm going to press into God's identity in hopes He will press into me a deeper understanding of my own. I have nothing to lose other than what I've already lost anyway...so it's all house money from here on out.

FIREFLIES

I've had this concept of sparks and lanterns stuck in my mind for months. I have no idea why. I can't tell you where it came from or why it seems to have planted itself so firmly into my mind and heart. Call it a divine download, maybe. Or at least that's what some part of me wants to hope it is. I don't know what it is about sparks exactly, but I find them totally mesmerizing. There's something so insanely brilliant about watching a stream of sparks cascade from the blade of a grinder as it presses into steel. It's a menagerie of friction, pain, danger, heat, violence, beauty. The spectacle only lasts for a moment, though. As fast as the sparks seem to explode, their light burning their way into our retinas, they disappear. The lights go out. As quick as they come, they go.

Kind of like us.

Our lives are but a vapor.[2] As soon as we come, we're gone.

It's quite depressing really. To think just how small we really are. Think about it. Our planet is but a particle of dust in a galaxy in a universe too big for words. Created by a God so big our minds explode as we try to merely catch a glimpse of understanding.

If our world is but dust, what does that make us? Dust of dust?

I'm staring out the window of a plane as I write this. Our lives look like nothing but pin lights on a pitch black canvas. From here, dust of dust of dust even seems more accurate.

It's starting to feel a bit like *Inception* (for all the Leo fans out there).

The point is, we are dust.[3]

And if that's true, then what? If we're mere sparks violently thrown from the blade of an unforgiving universe, what's the point?

Thinking about the apparent inconsequentiality of our lives makes you want to stand up from your nine-to-five prison of a cubicle, find the nearest beach, throw down a towel, and enjoy the sunshine while you still have a chance. It makes me wonder why I strive so much to "do" whatever it is I even think I "need" to do. I mean, why the heck am I even pouring all these hours into writing these words? It all seems so pointless when you think about it.

But is it all pointless? There has to be a point, right?

I hope there is.

I think it all hinges on how we look at things. Again, it all comes down to perspective. In the case of the spark, we get so enthralled with the violence, the blinding fire of it all, we forget to look back and see what came of that long-forgotten steel.

Isn't the steel the entire reason the grinder's lashing around in the first place?

The truth is, much of my life has been marked by complete forgetfulness that the steel even exists. I cruise through life oblivious to the cosmic universe that is hurling all around me. In my own mind, I am the master of the universe — and by "the" I mean "*my*" universe.

We all do.

And it's hard to comprehend the eternal implications of our decisions when we spend our days focused on the pinhead that is our life. And the more the cataracts sets in, the easier it becomes to cast off our importance as nothing more than a passing spark. But it's only half true.

Our lives are sparks. That's absolutely true.

But, what all those sparks leave behind, what our lives leave behind, does matter.

We may not always take the time to turn and look, but I think we would be pleasantly surprised by what we would see. Because what's left in the wake of such intense violence, struggle, pain, is something even more remarkable:

Polish.

Transcendent, enduring, timeless *brilliance*.

How does that work?
How does brilliance emerge from seemingly utter chaos and destruction?
From the collision of such minuscule and insignificant particles?
How can children dying in the clutches of hunger and poverty, broken marriages, lost jobs, cancer, AIDS — pain —

leave behind brilliance?

It seems so counterintuitive. Impossible. It really messes with your brain. It really challenges your heart and your beliefs about who this God who made us is.

It seems like the more I search for answers the only thing I get is more questions.

God's funny like that.

I mean, what is a spark exactly?

Maybe a definition would be a good place to start. According to the dictionary, *a spark is a glowing particle that emits light.*

But a spark doesn't just emit any light. It's intensely bright. Burn-your-retina bright. It's blinding. Undeniable. In that moment of inception, the moment the blade catches, the power of the friction that sets the sparks flying is overwhelming. But even more powerful is a spark's ability to ignite. A spark is the inception, the catalyst, the alpha, of a flame. The alpha of a life really. We always think of those catastrophic moments in our lives as the end of the story.

But the reality is that they are the *beginning.*

Our stories are defined by the moments that set our lives ablaze. Those are the moments that make us who we are. Those are the stories worth telling. Not because they are stories of tragedy, of pain, but because they are the birth stories of our *redemption.*

They are the stories of lives set on fire by a loving God who is consumed with a burning desire to light the world with the human heart.[4]

We are explosive beings designed in the image of an extravagant Creator with power beyond our capacity to fathom. And I can say without reservation that there is nothing more beautiful than a life caught on fire by the persistent love of God.

In our fallen mess, we *need* to be broken open. It's the only way.[5] The sparks of our lives define us because sparks ignite us. They ignite the lanterns of our hearts. Hearts designed to carry the glory of God's love to the ends of the earth.[6]

It's an amazing image.

But there's a problem.

Or at least I seem to have a problem.

A consuming one.

The problem is that *carrying* light and *creating* light are entirely different things. We are lanterns, conduits, carriers, of light, but despite our efforts, we cannot create it. The flame must come from outside ourselves. But I forget. We forget. And what results is me spending my life desperately attempting to convince myself that I am capable of creating the flame I long so deeply to carry. But over and over again, I fail. I burn out. And my world goes dark. And in the midst of the darkness I can never figure out why.

But, with perspective, the why isn't too difficult to see.

We are not created to carry our own glory. We are lanterns, ever longing to carry the light of our Creator *through* who we are and *through* our creativity.

It's a subtle yet critical distinction. It's hard to admit it, but truthfully, I've spent the vast majority of my life (if not its entirety) creating, achieving, succeeding, and working for the futile sake of my own glory. I've spent my life striving to create light and power with my own hands, desperately trying to fulfill the deepest longing we all have as humans: to carry glory. And tragically we waste our lives selfishly, obsessively, trying to create our own glory in the face of pure glory Himself, our Creator.

And in our obsession, we reject Him.
And in our rejection of Him, we forfeit our true selves.
And instead of our lives reflecting the brilliance of God's story, we burn out.

Like fireflies.

LANTERN

I am a lantern.
Glass stained, opaque.
Shrouded by the burns,
Of flames not wishing to stay.

A once vibrant kaleidoscope,
Cascaded in every direction,
Now lays solemn and dim.

Longing to illuminate, to shine.

But the flame never lingers,
Never radiates longer than a spark.
The flame is not my own.
It cannot come from within.

A blessing I can receive,
A gift I can give,
Yet not one I can create.

Absent of reciprocity,
Desires to burn die slowly.
Wisps of fading tomorrows,
Swept away by finalities.

The light destined to reflect,
I am overflowing with joy.
But in the wake of foresakenness,
I am dealing in the vastness of myself.

Empty of my only purpose,
Void of my only desire,
Lost in the longing,
Of what can only come,
From somewhere outside myself.

And to give of the flame,
Only another lantern may receive.

TWO
CREATIVITY

"Every child is an artist. The problem is staying an artist when you grow up."

—Pablo Picasso

BROAD STROKES

I'm left-handed. Some say that left-handed people are supposed to be more creative than right-handed people. Does this mean that right-handed people are supposed to be less creative? This can't be true. I know a lot of right-handed people who are incredible artists and amazingly creative. I also know that while I was growing up my mom was terrified because left-handers were supposed to have horrible penmanship, and, as a result, would be destined to a life of academic struggle. Turns out that I have beautiful handwriting. I also turned out to be a valedictorian.

Funny how that works.

I say all this because I find it interesting how good society is at defining us, caging us like animals at a zoo, predetermining our fates, long before we even have a chance to discover who we truly are. Despite the inaccuracies, a lot of us internalize these generously given definitions. Like self-fulfilling prophecies, we become them. The problem, though, is that society has an equally amazing way of being dead wrong. Society doesn't admit it's wrong, though. Instead, it throws a fresh label our way: *different*. And once we get labeled "different," everyone must rush to counsel us, discipline us, medicate us — "fix" us.

I read an article years ago that said there were some thirteen different personality/learning types commonly seen in children. It also said our educational system only caters adequately to two. Seriously. Two out of thirteen. Seems like a problem, right? So what happens to the kids who fall into the other eleven buckets?

We tell them they are broken.
We tell them they are dumb.
We tell them they have A.D.D.

And the saddest part is they believe us.

Then we give them a bottle of pills to "fix" them. A daily reminder, a ritual, to drive home their newly adopted identity.[1]

Spiritual death by a thousand decisions.

These are just a couple of examples. But the reality is, if we're not careful, the world is happy to tell us who we are. In the world's eyes, I am nothing more than a member of a marketing demographic, a trend, a tally in a survey, an employee on payroll — a data point on some graph that has been rolled into a best-fit curve.

The world may know a bit about *us*, but the world knows absolutely nothing about *me*.

We as a society love to paint in broad strokes. Anyone who's ever spent time in a laboratory knows that raw data is messy. Most of the time it's indiscernible. It doesn't make any sense. The shear volume and utter chaos of mile-long rows of figures is overwhelming. So we paint the world with large brushes. We summarize, standardize, average. It's convenient. It's easy. It's clean. But painting in broad strokes is dangerous when it comes to people because we are not trends. We are individuals. We are the specific data points that make up all those best-fit curves.

Generalizations serve their purpose, but their purpose is not to tell us who we are as individuals.

Despite its opinions, the world tells me nothing about who I am. It hasn't been right about me in any way. As a result, I've had to learn how to turn off my eyes and ears to a world that is still convinced that I should have horrible penmanship. That I should have a nine-to-five job. That I should just be happy with my 2.3 kids and a minivan, and work hard every day so I can send them to the best college in the country. Or in other words, pursue the American Dream.

But there's a problem.

I'm not even sure I want two kids (let alone an extra one third of a kid), and I definitely don't want a mini-van. I also don't believe in spending $250,000 on a college degree (yes, even though I have one)[2] or believe spending my days in a cubicle until I'm sixty qualifies as living. But this is what the world is relentlessly selling me every time I read the paper, watch TV, or go online.

What happens when I'm not buying what the world is selling?

Where does that leave me? What does that say about me? Am I deranged? Crazy? Foolish?

Most likely.
Definitely.
Probably.

I'm likely some gradient of the above, but the sad truth is, despite my desires to reject it, I've spent the vast majority of my life trying to catch my identity by buying into that mess — and I've learned the hard way that when I buy in life becomes exactly that, a mess. I don't want that life anymore. I don't think any sane person would.

So maybe I'm not crazy after all.

At least that's what I keep telling myself.

I have to keep telling myself because rejecting any of the paradigms our world is pitching seems to cause the entire system to break. Everything falls apart like a house of cards. Most of us can't even imagine a life without the societal and psychological structure we've been conveniently given. We are so programed through our childhood and adolescence to accept that "this is how the world works." But what if the world only works that way because we choose for it to behave in a certain way? Life is a mirror, remember? If that's really true, can't we choose instead to live in a world, live a life, that speaks deeply to the story for which our hearts are begging?

Steve Jobs spoke to this in a now-famous interview many years ago:

> When you grow up you tend to get told the world is the way it is. And your life is just to live your life and try not to bash into the walls too much, try to have a nice family life, have fun, save a little money. That's a very limited life. Life can be much broader once you discover one simple fact, and that is: Everything around you that you call life was

made up by people that were no smarter than you. And you can change it. You can influence it. You can build your own things that other people can use. Once you learn that, you'll never be the same again.

So if it's possible to define our life for ourselves, why don't we?

One word: *fear.*

We are terrified. Reject one fundamental facet, and the entire thing crumbles in our mind. The thought of it paralyzes us. It's all we've ever known. It's all we've ever been told. We don't even know how to create another vision of life because the vision has always been handed to us.

A lifetime of following along has allowed our independent and creative minds to atrophy.

We completely forget that we have the ability to imagine something different, to live in a way that is drastically different than the version we've been sold. And because we've abandoned our creativity, we can't imagine an alternative. So we fear the space our creativity should be filling. Then we listen to everyone else as they urge us to fall back in line, and we fear it even more. And we fear not because the alternative, the opportunity, is bad; we fear because the unknown, the uncertainty, the possibility of failure, paralyzes us.

It's like a pitch-black cave, nobody wants to go in without a flashlight.

Yet that's exactly what life demands of us. Sadly, though, most of us choose instead to live empty lives with our eyes wide shut — afraid of what may become of us if we drift outside the lines that have been drawn around us.

If we truly internalize the present reality that our lives are not what we were designed for, it forces us into that fear, presses us into a greater reality: *The life we were designed for is out there, somewhere — and the only way to find it is to step into the darkness.*

YOUTHFUL THINKING

I've never had a problem identifying myself as creative. Yet despite me telling myself (or anyone that asks for that matter) that I am creative, the truth is, my life rarely reflects my self-attributed creativity. When I woke up at age twenty-two in the midst of my broken life, I didn't know who I was. I didn't know where I was going. All I knew was that I didn't want to be who I, and where I, was. I couldn't even remember who I *used* to be.

In the search for anything solid, I wandered through many things. I felt like I was playing a life-sized version of Guess and Check. I didn't have a clue what to do, so I just started trying things. It felt a lot like wandering through a world-sized, pitch-dark room trying to find the light switch. I spent days, months, years, slamming into walls, looking for hints, hoping my eyes would adjust to the lack of clarity. I read about a billion books. I threw myself into music and wrote hundreds of songs. I wrote thousands of pages worth of journal entries, as my soul tried to find itself in the tranquility and vastness of a blank page. I went through job after job where I did everything from sales to marketing to engineering. I tried to start two companies. I tried everything. And failed every time.

It was my version of Exodus.[3]

And ironically enough, my journey, too, started in the desert. Only my desert was the Las Vegas strip.

I was aimlessly stumbling through life, hoping that one day I would arrive by process of elimination or just plain luck, because as much as I'd tried to figure out who I was, I still didn't have the slightest idea. Even conversations with friends and family didn't seem to help. None of them seemed to understand why I was so unhappy, so incompatible with life. No one could understand why I left the degree, the job, the promotion, the money — all of it. In their minds, I'd walked away from everything I'd ever worked for, everything my parents had worked and paid for to put me there — everything everyone had always wanted *for* me. In their minds I was crazy.

I distinctly remember sitting on the back patio of my parents' house with my dad and one of his good friends talking about what I was doing. I had recently moved home and I told his friend I wasn't looking for a job because I was trying to start a company. Without hesitating his friend replied, "You need to get your shit together, get off your ass, and get a fucking job."

The comment shook me, and stuck with me for a long time.
It really had me wondering if what I was doing what truly as
stupid as he seemed to think it was.

From the outside, I can see how it would seem absurd,
all the decisions I was making. The decisions were crazy.
I totally understand why he said what he said. I would
probably have told myself the same thing had I been in
his seat. But on the inside, whether I realized it or not,
and despite everyone's opinions, I was doing everything
I could to save myself from the living death I was feeling
inside. The world couldn't see it, but I could feel it. My soul
was withering. And the craziest thing I could think of was
spending another minute in a life I absolutely hated. In my
heart, there wasn't an option. I needed to escape the life I'd
trapped myself in.

I was on spiritual life support.

Things have been trending upwards for me in the three
years since I first left Las Vegas and spent a year wandering
through life in Northern California. I'm a little scared to even
say things have been good because saying so will probably
cause my life to fall apart tomorrow. I guess I'll cross my
fingers and see what happens.

In those years, I miraculously met the love of my life, dated
her, and married her in my hometown of Auburn, California.
I'd spent my entire life praying that God would bless me
with my soul mate. Only in God's humor would he put her
ten minutes down the road for the vast majority of my
life and yet not introduce us for fifteen years. I guess He
needed to prepare me to take care of such a precious gift.

Jessica is the best thing that has ever happened to me. We met when I was at rock bottom and yet, in some way that I still can't comprehend, she saw through the coffee shop apron and saw something in me that I couldn't even see in myself. Something that I'm still not so sure I see even now. She gave me something to work for, to live for.

She gave me a reason to love life again.

Blessed by her love, and a series of divinely opened doors, I was able to somehow transition from a career in real estate development to technology and product design. And as I write this, I'm now living in San Francisco and have been blessed with the opportunity to design products for some of the most respected companies in technology.

God's providence is beyond surreal.

What's most incredible to me is the speed at which God seemed to restore my life. I feel like He made up for all that I had lost in half the time it took to strip my life away in the first place.

I've always said I believe that God has a way of getting us to exactly where we need to be regardless of how lost we've been — and in my case, God proved me right.

I think the best kind of life is a life for which we can't take any credit. It leaves us with no one to point to except for God Himself.

The fact that my life is what it is today is nothing short of a miracle and the result of absolutely nothing of my own doing. I haven't deserved a single job I've had in the past three years. I've been ridiculously under-qualified for every one of them. Somehow the people who've hired me haven't seemed to notice. I am humbled by the opportunities God has granted me.

I am living proof that God is a lover of prodigals.

Yet, to be honest, as positive as the overall trend has been lately, and as much credit my mind gives to my Maker, deep down it has felt more like the result of the inevitable process of elimination than it has of me truly learning more about who I am or about my Creator. Yes, there has been some progress, and His grace and provision are beyond obvious, but the truth is, I think I've just gotten a little bit better at falling forwards instead of falling backwards.

I've been trying to trust Him in my blindness more than I ever have. It's still not very much, but I'm trying, and life does feel different. I feel different. Slowly, things have changed and continue to change. The variance is still nauseating at times, but at least the trend is seemingly on an uptick. This is one case were the best-fit curve serves a good purpose. A little glimpse of progress in the chaos helps quiet our heart's resistance to God's ever-loving process.

For a moment at least.

I know that leaning on God is the heart of the human experience, but I just don't believe life can be as miraculous as it's supposed to be if I don't know who I am. I haven't relented in searching for the truth I know is buried in my heart. I'm determined to find the small precious diamond God has been pressing, grinding, polishing, all these years.

Part of me believes we can't find ourselves sometimes, because the selves we need to find aren't ready yet. Either by our own sabotage or God's divinely perfect timing, we're somehow not ready to become that person. Maybe I'm missing it. Or maybe God's still grinding away on it.

Most likely it's both.

Even then, I can't seem to escape the reality that much of my life fails to reflect who God designed me to be.

I woke up to this reality late last year. Or I should say, God woke me up. In a totally random sequence of events, I was given the incredible opportunity to collaborate on a project with one of the most renown product design consultancies in the world, IDEO. To kick off the project, we all met together for an entire day at their Palo Alto, California, campus. It's the most creative place I've ever experienced. Nothing comes close. The air is filled with this undeniable energy. You can't escape it. The culture, the space, the people, the entire thing is contagious.

In the face of such creativity, I realized how much the incredible experience I was having couldn't be any further from the life I was creating for myself. In the contrast, I could see all that I was *not* doing. I realized that somewhere along the way I'd completely lost touch with all of the things I absolutely adored in my youth.

I'd completely lost touch with my creativity.

In the epiphany, I felt as though a massive door unlocked in my soul. A door I had closed a long, long time ago. A door life had closed somehow. A door to a room that held all of my passions, all of me.

In that moment, I realized that an immense part of who I was designed to be was connected to the creativity I'd somehow muted in my heart. Deep down I loved to design, draw, build, collaborate, develop ideas, write, play music — and most were barely visible (or completely absent) in my life.

It was a wake up call.

A tragedy, really, as I realized how much of myself I had lost in the transition from adolescence to adulthood.

I know the world is screaming at us otherwise, but I don't think we are ever supposed to grow up. I think what we call growing up is really just the gradual and steady abandonment of who we really are — a transfusion of who we are with who the world wants us to be.

We are never supposed to lose our youthful thinking.

I don't think we are ever more in touch with ourselves, our identity, our passions, our dreams, our heart, than we are when we are young. Why? In our youth, we have two things we lose when we become adults: innocence and freedom.

I think God's version of our life is infinitely more visible in our innocence and freedom. In our youth, we are not compromised by the pressures of a world tainted with the struggles we create for ourselves later on in life. In our youth, we are free to fully explore and express who we are. In the swelling of knowledge, achievement, and failure, that comes with the passing of years, His vision for our lives becomes ever more dim.

IDEO helped me do the most important thing I've ever done: rediscover my youth. And in my youth, I rediscovered my creativity. And when I started to unpack my childhood passions, a single, distinct message burned itself into my heart — a message that has always been there, but I had long forgotten:

I am creative. I am an artist.

A MOMENT FOR TRUTH

I am creative. I am an artist.

I think it's important to pause and unpack this truth, because deep down below my belief in my creative self is an even more profound truth: *this is true for all of us.*

We are *all* creative. We are *all* artists.

Now I know a lot of people are going to immediately disagree with me on this one, but I think the simplest way to come to agreement that we are all creative is to dive into Genesis 1:27:

"God created man in His own image..."

One of my favorite things about our God is that He is profoundly succinct. In only seven words, our God lays out the true essence of our identity. There's an oft-referenced quote that goes something like, "To know where you're going, you need to know where you've been." I think it's analogous in that we can tell the most about ourselves from the One who created us.

Why?

We are created in *His* image.

Just think about that reality for a moment. It's astounding. Incomprehensible really. Someway, somehow, God has imparted Himself into our design, into us. We are mirrors, reflections, of our Creator. So, to me, it seems that the deeper we dive into intimacy with our Creator, the more we are going to come to understand ourselves.

So let's break down Genesis 1:27 a bit more and see what emerges.

We only need to read the first two words of this verse to learn something profound about God:

"God created..."

Our God is a creator.

Now couple this with the end of the passage and we learn something equally profound about ourselves:

"...man in His own image..."

Our Creator created us in *His* likeness. In *His* image.

Being a creator is central to what it means to be human because being a creator is central to God being God.

God creates, so, in turn, we create. Every fiber in our soul is connected to this identity, to this innate desire to create. Whether we see it in ourselves or not, we are creators through and through.

We are *all* creative.

Spend a sunset staring up in awe at the Grand Teton Mountains as they tower over the winding, glassy waters of the Snake River in Jackson Hole, Wyoming, and it's undeniable that our God, our Creator, is in love with beauty. The entirety of creation drips in it — the result of God's overwhelming creativity and love.

It's easy to look narrowly at the word "artist" and conclude, "Yes, obviously, God's an artist, but believe me, I'm no artist. I'd be lucky if I could scratch out a stick figure!" But this reaction emerges from a narrow definition of what art is.

We need to ground our definition of "art" in its true and transcendent meaning:

Art is the output of an act of creativity.

And creativity isn't restricted to just visual expression. Our lives are continuous acts of creation, from painting a picture, to delivering a moving speech, to helping someone who's broken find hope, to a father reading his daughter a bedtime story. With every breath, we are ever shaping our world. Each moment carries the promise of a more beautiful and meaningful tomorrow. And we mustn't forget that each of us carries the power to create because we have been created by the ultimate creator and purveyor of beauty in the universe: God.

We are *all* artists.

VIGNETTES

> **vignette [vin-yet]:**
> *a short impressionistic scene that focuses on one moment or gives a trenchant impression about a character, an idea, or a setting and sometimes an object.*

I've been thinking a lot about the concept of vignettes lately. It's not a common word, yet we encounter them constantly without even realizing it. Vignettes are the thirty seconds out of a two-hour movie that stick with us. They are the hook in a song that we hum for days on end. They are the indelible moments of life and memories of people that we carry with us into old age.

Vignettes are the moments that matter.

But why?

These rare moments matter, because in them lies truth, an untarnished glimpse into who we are. They stick because they are succinct. They are honest. They capture us in those rare moments when our guard is down.

Deep within us, these moments, these acts of authentic creation, connect us. They move us. They speak to something greater.

Creation that is disconnected from its creator leaves us with nothing of who they are. And thus, it means nothing. Maybe that's the key. Creation only means something when it carries with it an innate glimpse into, a piece of, the heart of the creator. Anything less than pouring out our souls into the act of creation is empty. Just like our Creator, we *must* create in our own image.

The "what" is nothing without the "who."

If everything we do is art, then everything we create carries with it a vignette about who we are, who we are becoming, who we want to be, who we wish we weren't. The vulnerability of creation is utterly terrifying. And it's in this act of honesty, nakedness, that we allow the world a glimpse into our soul — in all its glory, in all its brokenness.

Adding to the pressure, we don't always know what our soul wants to reveal when we create. Sometimes we get to experience the revelation side by side with the world. And every time we have no idea how the world will respond to our confession, if at all.

I remember the night in college when I posted the first

song I'd ever recorded to *MySpace* (yes, I know I'm dating myself). I was so nervous when I pressed the "upload" button that I almost vomited. I didn't sleep the entire night. But when the morning came, whether they were telling the truth or not I'll never know, my friends had nothing but supportive and encouraging things to say. In the end, it didn't matter whether the song was actually good or not, because what I had created carried with it something my heart desired to communicate. And in honoring that desire in the face of the fear, I grew closer to who God is calling me to be.

In the years since that first song, I've shared many more songs and projects. I can tell you that those feelings of fear never go away. Every act of creation brings with it a renewed sense of trepidation. There's so much risk in creation it's hard to express. It's only in the act of creating that we're able to truly understand the whirlwind of emotions that rise up within us. It terrifies us to the deepest levels, yet there is something so liberating in the honesty. Succumbing to the fear, we risk killing ourselves from the inside out. While allowing the revelation, we risk condemnation from the outside world. But somewhere between the opposing evils lies the transcendent beauty that we find in honest, sincere brokenness.

Vulnerability is so inspiring, so incredibly moving because in the honesty, we all see and acknowledge the same vulnerability, fear, and deep longing for beauty and connection that exists in every one of us. In those moments, we realize we are not alone.

There is something more to this life than what meets the

eye. We are all connected, all part of the same beautiful story God is ever shaping and revealing to us. All creation carries with it vignettes that tell us something about the creator. And our Creator is telling us something deeply true about Himself through the crown of His creation, us.

I USED TO BE A PERFECTIONIST (THE DEVIL'S IN THE DETAILS)

I used to be a perfectionist.

But as I grew up my perfectionism faded as I slowly lost touch with everything that I cared about. It was essentially gone by the time I made it to high school. Another casualty to "maturity," I guess.

When I was young, I was exacting. By the time I reached college, "good enough to get the A" was my favorite quote. Excellence for the sake of excellence was a joke to me. It had been so long since I'd had a mere glimpse of passion about anything that "good enough" became good enough. The result: I spent my years building an empty and inconsequential life full of "accomplishments" I couldn't care less about.

I often hear people reference (myself included) the phenomenon that is the quarter-life crisis.[4] They say it's the cause of being released abruptly into the real world ill-equipped, without real-world skill. There is an element of truth in this definition. Yet, to me, the effect is the result of a more elemental cause: we forget what we care about.

I think we have a natural tendency as humans to drift. I also think the world is eloquently and profoundly subtle in its ability to separate us from our passions. Is it Satan? Yes. Is it our own humanity? Absolutely. We drift from our passions like boats loose from our moorings, and just as quickly as we lose them, they are replaced with heavy, cumbersome, draining things like duty, responsibility, achievement, obligation, and performance.

In a fraction of a second, life is gone.

I love the quote from Rob Bell's book *Love Wins* where he states, "Heaven for Jesus wasn't just 'someday'; it was a repent reality...eternal life is less about a kind of time that starts when we die, and more about a quality and vitality of life lived now in connection to God."[5]

He goes on to elaborate around the reality that our lives *now* are eternal, in the sense that we experience temporary (though potentially permanent) intense moments and seasons of life outside the context of time. In moments of great joy and great sorrow, time seems to evaporate from existence. The core of his thought is that maybe when Jesus is talking about finding eternal life (or on the contrary losing ourselves to eternal damnation) the reality of its existence is not something to hope for tomorrow, but ours to choose here today.

So it's with that thought in mind that I say the moment we lose our passions is the same moment we embrace a life of present and eternal unhappiness, of Hell. This also means we can find Heaven the instant we point our hearts in the pursuit of our passions. The moment we choose our creativity. The moment we choose God and the life He's ever calling us to.

The subtleties between Heaven and Hell are truly minute. The dividing line is nothing more than a hairline fracture in the sidewalk, so inconspicuous it's hard to even know which side we're standing on. So often we think of the differences as obvious, but the devil is truly in the details.

Yet in all the subtlety lies an incomprehensible polarity I don't think we can fully fathom this side of eternity. There is no mediocrity in Jesus' perception of the universe. The water is either hot or it's cold.[6] We spend our lives oscillating between happiness and misery, life and death, Heaven and Hell. And, over time, the variance begins to take shape, an invariable momentum builds, and the current carries us away. Every moment is a tug-of-war between the gravity of the world our past decisions have created and the ever-present passions in our hearts. Every moment is a seemingly unimportant choice to chase or give up on the life we were designed to live.

But the truth is, eternity lies in every moment.

Heaven and Hell are two sides of the same coin.

Every second of every day presents us with the opportunity to choose the incredible life God is ever offering us — or the freedom to reject it.

The differences between a full life and an empty life are much smaller than we think. Every choice matters. Because time has the uncanny ability to compound the effects of our decisions. And it's not until time has caused our life's trajectory to ramp that we come to grasp the consequences of the millions of decisions we've made.[7] This is why my life seemed to explode all at once. It seemed sudden, but it really wasn't. The reality was, the millions of decisions I'd made in my life had finally reached a tipping point.[8] And the cumulative product of my life finally gave way.

Our present circumstances are the product of yesterday's choices.

This is why it's so important for me to begin everyday clearly focused on which side of eternity I'm choosing to pursue. Without the conscious understanding of the results all my small, innocent choices will ultimately bring someday, I am lost. Choosing to follow my heart, my passions, my Lord, every morning before I have to make a decision about anything else in my life is making all the difference. I feel like my creativity is beginning to blossom again because I'm choosing to be creative everyday. Or more specifically, I'm choosing a life that allows my creativity to exist. I can't guarantee I'm going to make the right decisions every time, but I can absolutely guarantee what the trend of my decisions will look like because I choose to fight for my life and my heart and my creativity every single day. I know who I'm fighting for and I'm armed with a conscious filter to make sense of every decision I make.

Jesus wasn't kidding when He said the road is narrow.[9] Heaven and Hell are of the same coin; they are both found at the end of the same road. In our obsession with the eternal destinations of Heaven and Hell, we've lost sight of the truth that it's only in the posture of our hearts that they exist. Heaven and Hell exist in every moment. They are not mutually exclusive. They mix like rising and falling winds in the heart of a summer thunderstorm. There's power, beauty, danger, brutality, and brilliance in the dance. A product of our humanity, our lives are a melting pot of every side of eternity. The turbulence makes it so difficult to know what we're experiencing because as much as Heaven and Hell are different, they are eerily similar. And in the moment Hell can appear deceivingly alluring because it doesn't look all that different from Heaven. This is why choosing the direction of our hearts before the world has a chance to choose for us is essential to living a life in pursuit of God.

This may seem weird to say, but there's a part of me that is thankful for the ugliness of Hell because it makes the experience of Heaven that much more awe-inspiring. As much as we want to hate it, the truth is that one cannot exist without the other. They are symbiotic. The swirling and intertwining is truly elegant. In my heart the interplay feels much like the aurora borealis as the brightness of Heaven dances across the blackened canvass of Hell. As much as we hate to admit it, God's love for us and our ability to choose to love Him and ourselves only exist because of the polarity of life and death, love and hate, happiness and torment, freedom and slavery — Heaven and Hell.

If God (and everything He creates) is good, then Hell (in some way we can't fully understand) must be good, too.

It's easy to hate Hell. But, if we choose to open our eyes, there's beauty in the freedom Hell affords us. Mind-blowing beauty. The power of love lies in the freedom we have to choose to love, or not. Hell means God has given us the greatest power in all of creation: freedom.[10] So in this weird way that I don't fully understand, I find myself embracing Hell not because of what it is in-and-of-itself, but because of the essential role that it plays in the incredible story God is telling. I think denying the beauty of the polarity of our universe robs us of the opportunity to embrace the eloquence with which our Creator creates. There is such balance, fragility, intention, and necessity in every single detail. There is nothing wasted, nothing lacking.

Everything is good because everything is essential.

The devil is truly in the details. But the good news is that Heaven is, too.

STAY YOUNG, STAY FOOLISH.

"Stay young, stay foolish." — Steve Jobs

It's an often-quoted line these days, made famous in reference to the Stanford commencement speech the late Steve Jobs gave in 2005.[11] Yet, I think it holds the key for both staying connected to and rediscovering our passions.

Like I said earlier, I think our passions are the purest in our youth. When we are young, we are free. Free to fill our days with activities and things we love and enjoy. Yes, some of our likes and dislikes ebb and flow through the years, but I believe there are passions that are indelibly core to who we are as individuals, central to our beings, woven into our soul by our Creator with exacting precision and purpose. Our desires and passions exist because the God of the universe has an intention and will for our existence. There is something He desires to do *through* us.

And so our hearts and souls lie in the middle of the incessant struggle that exists between our loving God and our humanity. Life gets convoluted so quickly it's remarkable. Yet, with the same precision that made him revolutionary, Steve reminds us that our passions and purpose are easy to spot in our freedom and carefree youth. And it's in that freedom and playfulness that our creativity blossoms. But sadly, from the moment of our first breath, the world is hell-bent on trying to strip our passions from our lives — rendering us soulless and withered.

And that's exactly what happens.

If we let it.

Often we lose touch without even realizing it. The clues laid by our Creator are as obvious as we are blind. It's a timeless and painful dilemma. And so we wander, always searching for solace, yet rarely do we look back to the beginning, where the answers lie buried in the slipping memories of the days when we were young. The days when our hearts were free, our souls pure and innocent, our creativity and passions never more alive.

Our passions are the building blocks of who we are. All our creativity, abilities, talents, desires, and dreams emit from the passions woven in our hearts. It's in this reality that I realize why my soul has felt so barren for so long.

Everything that I am has withered because I have forgotten who I am.

It's impossible to be a perfectionist when your life is filled with nothing you care about — when you've forgotten who God designed you be.

It's only been recently in my reflection on the life and ideals that Steve stood for — his unwaveringly intense devotion to perfection, to creating things that were "insanely great" — that I realized what made him so profound: he had a clear understanding of the things he truly cared about. And he built his entire life around those core passions and devoted himself to expressing them to the fullest extent he possibly could. He was a perfectionist because he cared deeply about his life. Why? Because he was keenly aware of his passions, and vigorously filled his life with them. And it was out of this fullness of experience, of existence, that he created. Transcendent, moving, beautiful art can only come from this place of deep connection. Anything less is superficial. Transient. Dust.

Steve stayed young. He stayed foolish.

Further evidence to the power that exists when we create from our passions is an interesting study that was cited during the celebration of Steve's life at Apple headquarters the week after he passed.[12] The study analyzed the brains of people while using Apple products. They were hoping to determine why people seem so religiously "addicted" to their Apple devices. Yet they didn't find what they expected. When testing people while using their Apple products, instead of the brain activity concentrating in the area connected to addiction, users' brains were firing with activity from the exact location of the brain connected to *love*. Can someone be so deeply connected and in love with their passions that their creations emit the very same love?

Apparently so.

BE A VIGILANTE

> *"I wasn't willing to take enough steps back to move forward."*

I've been musing over the different things I thought I might have been passionate about in the past today. And the above quote is the conclusion I've come to. As I look back on the years, there are only a few things that seem to enduringly resonate within me. Even these few have waned and waxed through the seasons of life, but I attribute that more to my own oscillations than anything else.

There are simply times where the static is just too loud to hear the music.

But despite our soul's wanderings, and the world's shouting, our passions are always there — waiting to be discovered and rediscovered over and over again. It's interesting that our passions and greatness seem to be coupled by a single defining quality: *persistence*.

There's been quite a number of things that came to my

mind when I was trying to reconstruct my passions, yet, to be honest, I had a really hard time finding anything that passed the litmus test of persistence. What I mean is, in all the areas I thought I might be passionate about, my conviction always waned in time. Some lasted longer than others, but in the end, progress and growth demanded more than I was willing to give.

Throughout my life, I've been blessed with the ability to be good at quite a few things. I've been a good baseball player, basketball player, golfer, student, musician, designer, and writer. But I'm not exceptional at any of them. I'm not standout great. Do I believe I could be? Absolutely. If I have the ability, why am I not great at any of those things?

More often than not, I'm not willing to take enough steps back to move forward. I'm not willing to persist.

The million-dollar question, though, is am I not willing because they aren't a true passion of mine, or is it that I've simply lost touch with my identity? The first causes procrastination as we avoid doing something our heart truly doesn't want to do. The other is the tragic result of our own free will, blindness, and broken humanity.

I'm never going to be a professional athlete. That I know. I'm okay with that. Though in some ways it's disappointing to write the words. It doesn't feel good to kill off dreams that have consumed good portions of our lives. Is there still hope for me becoming a great musician, designer, writer, or entrepreneur? I think so. I am still pressing into those areas of my life and I'm curious to see what emerges. As it is with most things in this life, only time holds the answer.

I believe there are orchestrated times where the meaning of seemingly unconnected dots will explode into view. Maybe the passions are true and it's simply a matter of divine timing before everything comes to fruition. Deep down, though, I struggle with the angst of wondering if the time has come and gone and, in my blindness and brokenness, I've let my chances slip away. It's this angst that drives me today. I know that even though I may (or may not) have squandered an opportunity to create something "insanely great" out of my passions, those same opportunities present themselves anew every single day. So I'm doing my best to try and channel the angst into urgency and not let it paralyze me.

Each passing moment brings with it a conflict of emotion, though. Time brings confidence via knowledge and experience, but fear grows out of memories of the failure and apathy that have crippled my life. And all of it gets coupled with the ever-increasing stakes of the American Dream (i.e. things, bills, homes, jobs, family) and compounded by the ever-shortening runway that is our life.

Like that Anna Nalik song goes, "The hour glass is glued to the table."[13]

Whether we choose to admit it or not, the stakes are high. Life is demanding. There's no denying it. It's demanding whether we choose to follow our passions or not. And if life isn't hard enough already, a life in pursuit of our true selves is often the more demanding road.

In the face of all this adversity and fear, how do we persist?

The tipping point, I think, hinges on our connectedness to God and our identity. If we are following God and living out of our passions, living life any other way seems crazy. Lost and disconnected, padded by the illusion of the American Dream, taking the supposed risks to re-prioritize our life seems even crazier. But the craziness the world propagates is a lie. Passion and creativity only exist when we are in tune with God's version of us. If we choose the world's version of us, we become empty vessels, shadows, of who we could be.

The stakes are high.

We can't let our awareness of what's central to us slip away. God is the source of our passions and our passions are the source of our creativity — so we have to be vigilant in our pursuit of God and protection of who we are.

Don't know what your passions are? Try making a list of possible candidates. Spend time musing over the list. Let all the memories and experiences that have moved you deeply flow to the front of your mind and into your heart.

Remember what it feels like to care.
Remember what it feels like to be inspired.
Remember what it feels like to live for something.
Remember what it feels like to be young.

Those are the moments when we are truly alive.

We can feel those feelings again. We can create a life full of those moments if we have the courage, the conviction. If nothing seems clear, make the commitment right now to be vigilant about finding your passions. Stand for something. Even if that something is a desire to discover what that something is.

Be a vigilante.

SOME NIGHTS WE SOW. SOME NIGHTS WE REAP.

I was really moved by something Louie Giglio said on Twitter recently:

> Some nights we sow and some nights we reap, but we always work alongside a miracle-working Farmer in His beautiful field.[14]

There are times in life where the world seems to come at you at a million miles an hour. So fast you become absolutely overwhelmed with how amazing life is. Life is pouring out of you faster than you can even create it. Yet, almost as suddenly, the world can shift and feel like it's fleeting, running away, twice as fast as it came in the first place. Instantly, life becomes a brick wall and everything you are seems locked inside somewhere without a key. Everything inside of you wants to pour itself out, but it can't seem to find a way to escape. You want to create more than anything, yet your hands, mind, and heart are frozen.

Some nights we sow. Some nights we reap.

What is equally as fascinating is how something so

seemingly innocent and unexpected can be the key
to opening everything up. I'm listening to a new band
I stumbled across on YouTube today. A case of true
serendipity. I'm listening to their album for the first time as
I write these words, and for some unexplainable reason, it's
opening my soul up in this moment.

As much as my heart has wanted to, I've had nothing to
say or create for days, and yet here I am and this song just
seems to sing of this moment. It's echoing everything I feel
inside, and it's setting the urges in my heart free. Maybe
therein lies some cosmic secret, the key to unlocking an
imprisoned and hopeless heart: knowing someone else,
somewhere, some-when echoed the same feelings as you.[15]

The realization that we're not alone in the struggle, the
realization that we're all down here on our knees, crying out
to our Creator to rescue our hearts, to rescue our souls — to
release the indescribable ability to carry His raw power that
lies dormant inside our fallen humanity, is what unites us.

Just thinking about the perilous state of our world, you
can't help but feel God's tears, feel His broken heart. I don't
know what's more awe inspiring, God's creation or God's
unwavering, redemptive love for the broken mess we've
made of His masterpiece.

Some nights we sow. Some nights we reap.

Even God.

We're not alone. Our Creator feels our pain and hears
our cries on a deeper level than we can ever begin to

understand. And it's in that brokenness, in that desperate love, that God called Jesus to step from His throne, lay down His crown, and give everything to rescue all of creation — all of us. All because God refuses to lose. God refuses to give up the pursuit for the one thing He loves more than anything in the entire universe — us. Jesus gave up everything, even His divinity, to become a man, because that's what it took to meet us where we are. There's no length He won't reach, no place He won't go, to save us. We should be lost. We deserve to be lost. But our Creator is so madly in love with us that He gave everything to create a way home.

In Jesus we reap everything we've never planted. He takes our weeds, our famine, upon Himself, and gives us paradise.

Grace isn't fair, but that's why grace is so incredible. The beauty is in the discrepancy.

Think about it.

This.
Is.
Our.
Creator.

This is our father. This is our God.

How can we do anything but lay our faces on the ground and praise Him? How can we even fathom the price He's paid for us — His love for us? When we see Jesus for all He is, it's impossible to hold onto anything we think we are.

Without Him we are nothing. Yet *in* Him we find everything. We find the impossible, the unexplainable, the miraculous. And it's only in Him working *through* us that we do anything at all.

Some nights we sow. Some nights we reap.

But in a life lead by Christ, *every time* He sows, we reap.

GREATNESS (PAYING DUES)

We all want to be great at something. Greatness is wired deep within our spirit, and our hearts long for it. Our souls yearn to express themselves. To be discovered. To be realized.

We long to shine.

Yet, despite our universal longings, greatness seems so elusive. It seems almost exclusive, really, with most of us standing on the outside looking in as others step into the brightness of their true potential.

Our culture is fascinated with success. And even more so with this concept, or myth really, of overnight success — as everyone seems to explode into glory out of nowhere. At least this is how it's made to look. And because this is the story we're constantly being told, we have all come to believe we can achieve anything we want instantly. Somehow greatness has become something you flick on like a MacBook Air. And if greatness doesn't come instantly, we label ourselves as failures and fall back into mediocrity, broken like prodigals. We're victims of technology, media, our own envy — all of which are ever whispering in our ears that we deserve to be great *now.*

It's all Kool-Aid.

Our society has hijacked the American Dream. All the high schools, universities, news papers, commercials, TV shows, and movies are all hyping the same lie: *you can be anything you want to be, right now.* And in this false entitlement we swagger through life, faking it as best we can, while, deep in our souls, we're praying with fingers crossed that someday luck will pay us a visit. Or, we resent life for the greatness that doesn't come because we don't have the slightest clue what we're doing, or what it even means or takes to be great. From our years of indoctrination, all we know is that we *deserve* it. At least that's what we like to think.

But we don't deserve it.

Not in the slightest.

Most of us live our lives as though greatness is simply going to appear one morning out of thin air. But the truth is, greatness doesn't simply happen. It's not some whimsical fairy that decides to dust you with brilliance one night while you sleep.

There is no such thing as overnight success.

Sorry to burst the bubble, but it needs to be said.

Life is not a passive experience. There are no free rides. Life is simply an opportunity. An opportunity to discover and explore. An opportunity to grow. An opportunity to work. An opportunity to dig deep inside ourselves and discover the greatness that's woven into the very fabric of our being. But it's also our opportunity to waste, to forfeit — to ignore. Our opportunity to wait, to envy, to covet. That's the beauty and tragedy of our free will. Our Creator loves us so much that He's willing to entrust the entirety of the divinity we possess, the greatness woven deep inside us, to our own decisions.

Greatness is not an accident.

There's more truth than we can ever grasp in the old adage: *luck is simply when preparation and opportunity meet*. In our entitlement and ignorance, we love to tear down those who emerge from the ashes of mediocrity with the fire of a phoenix. We strip them of their accomplishments and who they've worked so hard to become, and worst of all, we call them "lucky."

Luck is not an accident, either. Luck is *created*.

Despite our obsession with the idea, luck has absolutely nothing to do with anything in this life. The sooner we accept this truth the sooner we can accept accountability for the lives we are creating.

Greatness is a choice.

Greatness is choosing to embrace the opportunity God is ever-offering us to grow and learn. It's the result of relentlessly seeking a deeper understanding of who we are and who God is calling us to be. Greatness means choosing every day to live lives consumed by urgency, fear, blood, sweat, tears, pain, late nights, early mornings, discipline, conviction — because that's what it takes. That's what God demands of us. It's about choosing perseverance and pressing ever deeper into our hearts, our longings, and trusting that there is a divine purpose in the pursuit. It's choosing to live with the reckless conviction it takes to pour out our souls over and over again to discover what the bleeding will make of us.

Greatness is about seeing the world (and ourselves) through a long-term lens. Greatness is about paying dues, not simply for due's sake, but because the deeper reality is greatness isn't actually about what we make; it's about what the discipline of creating and bleeding day in and day out makes *of* us.

As I write this, I'm flying the red-eye from New York to San Francisco. Jessica and I just spent the past ten days exploring the city and celebrating our one-year wedding anniversary. Before the trip, I bought a bag of fortune cookies from the Golden Gate Fortune Cookie Factory in San Francisco. If you ever have a chance to visit this place, do it. They're phenomenal. They make them fresh in a tiny warehouse tucked away in an ally in the heart of China Town. Anyway, I just popped open a cookie and the fortune was quite timely:

Many possibilities are open to you — work a little harder.

Greatness is truly about work. We are given divine talents, passions, skills — but the development of those gifts are *our* responsibility. We have to work for them. We have to work to become the vessels God desires us to be. We have to surrender our lives to Him. We have to endure the pain as He presses the grinder deep into our souls if we're ever to see the brilliance that is hiding below the surface.

Greatness is about persistence.

Last night, we caught up with an old friend of mine in the city who plays guitar for one of the most popular bands in the world right now, *Foster the People*. Their music is literally *everywhere* these days. Their rise to popularity has truly been meteoric. It's been incredibly fun to watch.

We wound up connecting in New York by random chance, as they happened to have a show in Central Park that overlapped with our trip. We grabbed last-minute tickets to the show and we met up afterwards at a rooftop nightclub in the city. As we were all standing there overlooking the Manhattan skyline at 1:30am, I told him how happy I was for him and how great it was to see all his hard work paying off because I knew how long and hard he'd been working to make a career in music. Looking out over the city he said (paraphrasing as best I can remember), "You know, I've been pursing music full-time for eight years now...and it really is a blessing to finally be in a place where I can do many of the things I've been dreaming about since I was a kid. But, you know, all of this, the success, this life, is truly surreal. Honestly, overwhelming at times. Our life is like this every night. Shows. Appearances. Bus rides. Plane flights. Every night we fall asleep in one city and wake up in another. After a while it all starts to run together...But, you know, as glamorous as this all seems on the surface, none of this is real...the success...this life we're living...this isn't real life...and it's so easy to get caught up in it and start believing that it is. That's why it's so important to always ground myself in that truth...there are times I miss real, day-to-day life, the routine...the depth of relationships it brings."

As he reminisced, what struck me most was that the success itself was almost too overwhelming to comprehend. To him, it was nothing more than a lie. A mirage. Nothing more than some strange product of him doing what he loves. The success was some detached reality that rose up in the wake of their talent, their greatness, and the true reality, the one he's holding onto, is the work, the persistence, the day-to-day grind of doing what it takes to get there, and stay there. The apparent success is nothing but swirling, ethereal noise. For him, his love for music, the work required to grow as a musician, and relationships with close friends and family are real life.

Those eight years of persistence and a lifetime of dreaming are his north star.

He chose to work a little harder. He persisted a little bit longer. He honed his craft and pressed into his heart and God's will for his life a little bit deeper. Every day.

Maybe he got the same fortune cookie as me.

And you know, his story isn't really all that unique. I'm sure his band mates' stories carry a similar arc. Remember, there's no such thing as an overnight success. They are great because of their years of persistence, because they fought for their creativity, their talents, their passions, their dreams. And because of their willingness to press violently deep into their identities, I had the blessing of watching the sun set over a Central Park stage on a blissful New York summer night to the sound track of one of the best concerts I've ever seen. And for the brilliance of the evening, and for the goose bumps I got during the epic crescendo of "Call It What You Want," I am forever grateful. To be honest, at some spiritual level I feel indebted to them for the musical gift they gave us last night. The same gift they give every night as they crisscross the globe blessing millions of people with the brightness of their creativity.

But as glamorous as their creativity's finished product seems, it's important to not lose sight of the truth that the persistence required to create it is anything but glamorous. Spending years locked in an apartment honing their musical skills, living most of their lives on a tour bus, is anything but glamorous. Every one of those guys misses being home. They miss their families. They miss their friends.

Creativity is truly a sacrifice. It's everything but glorious. Creativity is struggle. It's pain. It's friction. It's fear. It's loneliness. It's pressing forward into our blindness trusting in the story our hearts are longing to tell. And greatness is no different. It's working for months and years and decades to unpack our potential. It's struggling to perfect our creation only to throw it all away one foot from the finish line because we know that starting fresh is the only way to press deeper into what it can be, what it needs to be. It's obsessing over a single sentence for hours only to delete it entirely because the best it can be still isn't good enough.

We keep pressing because something in our soul tells us that anything less than complete resolution is worthless.

And it's true.

Even if the world thinks what we create is great, we know whether it truly is or not. We know if we left everything we had on the table. We know if what It Is and what it could be are one in the same. Greatness is being able to answer that question with a "yes." Creation is the repeated emptying of our souls, the incessant prying into our hearts, the constant rebirth of who we are, in search of the greatness we can feel burning inside us.

Or maybe that's the real divine truth: *surrendering ourselves to God is the only thing that can make us great.*

The selflessness of creativity is truly profound. When we create, we give of ourselves not for our own gain, but for the gain of others and for the glory of God. We give because we know what it feels like to experience and be blessed by greatness. We know what it feels like when our soul fills up our chest with inspiration as we experience the brilliance of Broadway, the crescendo of our favorite song, the taste of the finest cuisine that our palates have ever known.

Greatness lights our souls on fire.

And that brilliance is contagious.

It ignites this deep, profound desire within us to give that feeling to someone else. It overflows our hearts so intensely that we reflexively pour ourselves out for others.

My heart has been racing this entire week. I was in the presence of true greatness four times in two days. In two days, I had the blessing to experience the éclairs and croissants from the best pastry chef in the country at Almondine, cuisine from the best French chef in the country at Bouley, the best Broadway show in the world (*Lion King*), and one of the most amazing concerts I've ever seen (Foster the People).

My heart is so on fire that all I can think about is diving into anything creative my heart can find. I am so filled with the beauty of the creativity I've experienced that my soul is overflowing with inspiration and an unwavering conviction to press ever deeper into my own passions. I am so amped right now that nothing I'm writing even seems to do justice to the fire that's burning in my chest. The burning is so intense, the beauty I've witnessed so overwhelming, that the thought brings tears to my eyes. The desire for this inspiration to manifest itself is almost frustrating because everything that's pouring out of me seems nothing more than an echo of what it feels like inside. It's my prayer that some way, some how, these words are carrying more than how it feels to me in this moment; that someday my years of toil may give someone, someday, even the faintest glimpse of the awe inspiring inspiration I was blessed with this week.

I never want to lose this feeling. I feel like my soul is exploding inside my chest. I don't know if I've ever felt such a burning desire to be more than who I am as I do right now.

I wish I could live out of this moment forever.

Is it impossible, though? To hold on to this? Can greatness be somehow bottled in our hearts? Do we truly possess the divine ability to light each other's hearts on fire, and keep the flame lit?

I think so.

As long as it's the light of God we are carrying and not our own.

I think the key to keeping our souls on fire is the constant pursuit of beauty. We have to seek out those things that stir our souls and allow ourselves to be caught up in greatness any chance we get. We have to *want* it. We have to *long* for it. We have to *thirst* for it.

We can't forget how rare true greatness is. We have to give everything we have to seek it in our world and in ourselves. We have to be vigilantes. When we find it, we have to hold on to it. With everything we have. Like our lives depend on it.

Because they do.

We must never let go of the indebtedness we *all* have to burn brightly, to ignite one another with the light of God. We are called by our Creator to be an army of stars in a dark and broken world. The greatness our hearts are ever longing for is real. It's there if we choose it, if we seek it, if we pursue it, if we fight for it.[16] We as a generation have a choice to make. And whether we realize it or not, our souls are hanging in the balance.

So with a hopeful and desperate heart, embrace the fear, embrace the pain, embrace the hope, embrace the longing, pour out your soul over and over again in pursuit of everything you know you are, and seek greatness.

The world needs it more than you know.

THREE
FREEDOM

"Between stimulus and response there is a space. In that space is our power to choose our response. In our response lies our growth and our freedom."

—Victor E. Frankl

FREEDOM IS PROFIT

Today I am a professional writer. Not because I've made any money off my writing (which I haven't), but because I've been paid by a company to do a job that I've done in less time than I was given and I'm using my "free" time to write. It's an interesting reality because right now we're both winning. My freedom is free for them, and it's profit for me.

Freedom is profit.

The idea has my mind racing. I feel as though this idea has been buried deep down inside me and for some reason today has finally managed to burst through the surface of my psyche. When most of us hear the word "profit," our minds immediately think of money. And for many of us the money is the end result. But it can't be. It can't be, because money isn't real. Money is nothing more than an idea, an illusion, a piece of paper backed by nothing more than the collective idea of it's worth. If you think about it, money really isn't much of anything. Yet, for not being anything, it's become the linchpin of our planet. It is the central idea that drives everything.

But why?

Why do we place so much value on something that holds no real value?
Why do we give our lives to trying to accumulate as much of this ethereal currency as we possibly can?
Why are we willing to sell our souls for it?
Why are we so consumed by it?

Why am I consumed by it?

We are consumed by it because regardless of how real money is, money has *real* influence. And that influence is important. I think there are times that the Christian community can villanize money and make those that possess the gift of being able to create it feel guilty. And I don't think it's right. Money is neither good nor bad. It's agnostic. It can be used for good just as easily for bad. Money is simply a vehicle. A tool.

And it doesn't matter what our opinions are about money, because in the end, the truth is our world largely runs on it. That's why it's wasted breath to dispute, or attempt to villanize, or downplay money's importance.

Because it *is* important.

It's definitely not everything, but the truth is money is a lot of things. And because of the central role it plays, we can't afford to dismiss or ignore it entirely. We must learn to navigate in and around our world's dependence on money.

If the world were an engine, money is the oil. It removes friction and gives us the freedom to move. And more than the money itself, or its influence, it's the freedom that money affords us that I think our hearts are most fixated on. If we really think about it, everything we do isn't in the pursuit of money, it's *freedom*. Freedom from the world, from society, from each other, from ourselves.

We long for freedom because it is the greatest gift our God has given us. And we want as much of it as we can get. And we should.

We do many things with the worldly freedom that money affords us. We buy cars, houses, toys — things. We go on trips. We help others and pass on a small portion of our freedom to them. And all those things are nice in and of themselves, but even deeper than the empty things we can buy, money increases our freedom to create. People often say that freedom can be achieved without money. I disagree (at least in the physical sense of freedom). Without money, we may have freedom of time and freedom of influence, but true freedom, the kind of freedom creation demands, requires that and more. It requires the freedom to move (travel) and the freedom to leverage materials in our world (things). This quest for freedom, though, can be a slippery slope. If we're not careful, our pursuit for freedom can get woven into the destructive pursuit of control.

Freedom and control are not the same.

Freedom, in it's purest form, is an untethered state of being (mind, body, and soul) where we are able to fully experience who God is and limitlessly pursue all that He created us to be. It is in this freedom, the freedom we can only find in God, that the opportunity exists for us to deepen our understanding and expression of who we are and ultimately bear the fruit God has planted in us — because it is out of an intimate understanding of ourselves, our Creator, and an unwavering trust in His motives and our desires, that true, divinely-inspired creation emerges.

Freedom gives us the opportunity to engulf our lives with our passions and create from hearts overflowing with inspiration.

Yet, as beautiful as it all sounds, the unfortunate truth is, freedom has become quite elusive — as the state of our world can attest.

But why? Why does freedom seem to be so fleeting?

In the eyes of broken humanity, freedom is a commodity. We believe that in order to increase our own freedom, we must decrease another's. This is not true. Has the freedom I've created for myself today decreased the freedom of my employer? Absolutely not. Freedom is infinitely abundant. Freedom can be mutual. In fact, freedom *should* be mutual.

If it's not mutual, it's not freedom.

It's control.

SAYING "NO"

So how do we create freedom?

N. O.

Just two letters. Yet they may be the key to creating freedom — the freedom we need to be creative. Freedom is a choice. This means that if we are to choose freedom, we have to "not choose" something else.

We have to say *no*.

Saying no allows us to spend the majority of our lives operating from our core passions instead of losing our lives to an endless progression of empty obligations.

Saying no creates space.
Saying no creates free time.
Saying no allows us to spend our time focusing on the things that matter most.

It's a simple concept, yet few of us are actually able to do this. The few that do are the ones we talk about for decades, even centuries. They are the great innovators and leaders of our time. Why are they so impactful? They live lives full of passion, conviction, and purpose — lives empty of obligation. And how are they able to accomplish this?

They say no.

Why is saying no so difficult?

Saying no takes courage.

At heart, most of us are pleasers. We want to avoid conflict. We want to make others happy. We want things to be "smooth."

Passionate people are not pleasers.

They know their purpose and they do not compromise it for anything. They are vigilantes. Their purpose is their north star, their reason for existence, the keystone that holds the entirety of their life together. And they fight for it.

Our passions are incredibly hard to discover, yet remarkably easy to lose. The subtlest way we begin to lose our grip on our passions is saying yes to things outside of our purpose. Saying no is about identifying and holding tightly to the essential and casting out everything that isn't.

Our purpose is the signal.

Everything else is noise.

BE AN EDITOR

I watched an interview with Twitter founder, Jack Dorsey, some time ago and he made a comment that has stuck with me ever since. When asked what his role at Twitter is (he's the Chairman and CEO by title) he simply said, "I'm the editor."[1] In other words, his role is to say no. He is the most important person in the company. Steve Jobs' favorite word was "no." Great creators, artists, don't create unnecessarily. In their pursuit of purity, they create exactly what is needed. No more. No less. "Less, but better," as the great Dieter Rams so famously said.

It's really hard to be an editor.

Sometimes it means people will be unhappy. Editing out things, people, or their work is not fun. People have feelings. People get disappointed, hurt, embarrassed, offended. But it's okay if the truth hurts sometimes. Now I'm not saying go out and be brutally honest to the point where you're hurting people just for the sake of being honest. We are called to love one another relentlessly. Achieving honesty and diplomacy with the same breath is truly a tightrope walk. But I do believe it is possible. And it's necessary that we learn to find that balance. I think finding that equilibrium point is what separates great leaders from the rest. And when you combine that finesse with an uncanny eye for the essential and a humble, willing heart, a brilliant thing happens:

We become vessels for the glorious work God is ever-desiring to do through our lives.

This idea of being an editor is the key to freedom. Every time we say no to something that attempts to draw us away from our core self, we gain freedom and we are drawn deeper, closer, into our true identity. This freedom can come in an infinite number of forms, such as gained time, emotional energy, and creative inspiration. When I heard Jack talk about his perspective on life, my eyes were opened. I began to think of myself, too, as an editor, and I began to seek out areas in my life that I could edit. Every time I successfully "edit" something I feel so liberated. I'm still very much beginning the process of editing my life, though. It is a difficult process, because it's hard to differentiate between what truly matters and all the nonessential things we subconsciously say yes to everyday.

Yet, inch-by-inch, I feel like I'm gaining ground and slowly winning back my life.

EDITING MY LIFE

The first area I'm trying to focus on is my job. I figured it would be the best place to start because it is the most time consuming obligation in my life. Despite the fact that I like to design, and have been blessed with the opportunity to get paid to do it, it is very much an obligation creatively because I spend the majority of my week creating for *others* instead of for my own heart. It's a subtle but monumental difference.

Creative fulfillment comes from two things: The ability to create, and the freedom to create what our heart calls us to create. Right now I only have half of the equation and I'm on a quest to get the other. My intent is to eliminate as much unnecessary work or time commitments from my day as possible. This frees me up to spend more time in the areas I'm passionate about and/or on high impact tasks and projects for my employer. The result of this is two things: First, I will create better products for my employer that are focused and address what matters most. Second, I will spend less time doing work. Better results, in less time. This creates more value for my employer, and more freedom for me.

Win-Win.

To do this, I started by picking off some of the "low-hanging fruit": reducing the time I spend in meetings and eliminating unnecessary product features.

First, meetings.

My approach to most meetings is simple. I try not to show up. If it is not essential, I do my best to get a pass. Everyone thinks his or her meeting is important, but the reality is, most are not — or, at a minimum, are twice as long as they *should* be.[2]

When I do have to conduct a meeting, I try to set an aggressive time limit (usually thirty minutes max) and bring a pre-defined agenda. Everyone loves an hour meeting, but the truth is, it's mostly wasted time. Many of us spend the majority of our days at work *talking* about work.

This needs to change.

The company I work for instituted a great policy last week. They banned meetings on Tuesdays and Thursdays so we can spend less time meeting and more time executing.

They get it.

And the benefits are two fold: we meet less frequently and, when we do, it's for shorter periods of time. It's brought a sense of focus and a shot of energy to the entire organization.

Professionally speaking, I am a product designer. I design web and mobile products. This means the majority of my day is spent analyzing and prioritizing design and product feature requests and figuring out the best way to achieve the desired goal. I've come to realize that distilling a product down to its most essential and valuable features is incredibly difficult. As a result, most products are full of endless features that are really time expensive to create and offer minimal (if any) real value to the user. With this in mind, my goal is always to eliminate as much of the fluff as possible and only deliver on the elements that directly support the core purpose of the product.

A great product is designed with intention and only has what is needed. Everything else is distraction.

Creating great products isn't easy, because being an editor is hard. And it's hard because it takes more than just knowing what needs to stay and what needs to go. Being an editor is hard because it takes confidence, discipline, resilience, and focus.

I've found the easiest way to eliminate the clutter in a product is to simply get an understanding of the central goal, draw a firm line from point A to point B, and then eliminate anything that doesn't directly support that path. No matter what people may think, anything outside the central focus is minimally beneficial at best — and most of them are truly non-essential. It's not always easy to trust the truth of the last statement, but you have to believe it wholeheartedly.

I fail in this department vastly more often than I'd like to admit, but I try to do this with every project I'm given. I try to be decisive in my attempts to simplify the solution to the problem that's presented. Growth takes lots of time and persistence, but I believe that I can become a great designer if I press myself deeper into the art of being an editor, one day, one project, at a time.

What I find most interesting is, even though my employer

thinks they're paying me to design, the reality is they're paying me to say no. I actually don't attribute any of my ability to design things to the art itself. In my mind, the art becomes the inevitable result of saying no to the non-essential enough times. As you grind your way through the no's, the design becomes obvious.

It's my little secret.

One of my favorite "no" stories is the one about a marketing consultant who was hired by a large company to come up with a new slogan. They paid the consultant a six-figure sum to deliver the company's new brand. After a few weeks, the consultant came back and presented his results to the CEO where he revealed a three-word slogan. Initially, the CEO of the company was taken back. He couldn't believe he paid the consultant so much money and all he got in return was three words. When he voiced his frustration, the consultant simply replied, "You didn't pay me for the three words I chose; you paid me for the 10,000 words I didn't."

Our value, freedom, happiness, and fulfillment are directly proportional to our ability to edit the millions of little areas that make up our lives.

Work is an obvious and easy place to start. Others have proven to be a bit more elusive. It's hard to express just how hard it's been for me to try to learn to be a better editor. As much as I've been trying to edit my professional life, I still slip all the time and things get away from me.

I've been keeping mental track of the effects of not asserting myself, because, for me, finding a way to track my progress and results helps me see through the internal hesitancy that swells when we attempt to grow out of our natural tendencies. After tracking myself for the past couple months, I've come to a really simple conclusion about the costs of not being a good editor — it's expensive.

Situations where I do a good job as an editor are easily two to three times more efficient than ones where I do a poor job. For example, last week I did a really poor job of editing a project and instead of it taking eight hours to complete, it took twenty-four. I lost half my workweek because I did not have the courage to say no when it was fully in my power to do so. Sixteen hours of freedom, gone. Sixteen hours that were filled with frustration instead of fulfillment. Sixteen hours that I could have invested in these pages.

Lesson learned.

As time goes on, those types of situations seem to happen less and less. With practice comes confidence, I guess. I can say that the more I see the results, the more I'm able to resist the hesitant feelings that try to push me back into my old way of living. I'm also finding that the more I'm able to focus my life, the more connected I feel to God and my divinely-given identity.

Recently, I've started trying saying no to things in my personal life as well. I realized that much of my time outside of work was also spent on things that were largely outside of my passions. My weeks were being filled with people that weren't having a positive influence on me, events I didn't want to go to, or obligations that *seemed* important but really weren't. It's so easy to fall into the trap of thinking everything is important. But the reality is, a very small percentage of our lives hold the vast majority of the importance. The 80/20 rule is very, very real.[3]

And so I've begun creating more time in my life by eliminating much of the things that have been draining me emotionally or taking up (read: wasting) much of my free time. Time and energy that could be invested into those that I love and into my creativity and passions — into my purpose. It sounds selfish. And it is. But the truth is, God deserves the best of us. And being intentional about being our best is the only way. God created us to be ourselves, and so for me the best way that I can honor Him is to respect myself enough to protect who He's created me to be.

The biggest key to freeing up my personal life has been to be honest with myself about things I do not want to do, and to be open with those that are close to me about it. I've had to make a conscious decision to stop trying to please everyone all the time. For example, I'm very much an introvert. Highly social environments are really draining for me emotionally. I enjoy them when I have the energy, but most of the time they completely wipe me out. I get recharged by spending the day alone reading, writing, designing, playing music, or playing golf.

Solitude is my fuel.

Yet, despite knowing this, I realized that most of the time I would say yes to social outings even though, deep down, I knew I didn't have it in me to go. It's taken some courage, but I've started saying no to most of these types of things. It was hard to say no at first, but every time I do I feel liberated. I feel good that I've honored my heart and avoided something that would have done nothing more than created frustration, resentment, and exhaustion in my life. Plus, my less-than-enthusiastic attendance usually does a good job of zapping the fun out of the room for everybody else. As a result I've been much happier and I have more energy to devote to the things that truly fulfill me and more energy to give when I do choose to go to bigger gatherings.

I've been doing the same with my social circle. I've learned I do best with a small, yet really strong, group of friends. That's where I feel most fulfilled. As much as I wish I did, I don't have the social energy to manage a large network of friends. I'm just not gifted in that way. And it's okay.

I've stopped trying to juggle all the causal friendships and all the time that was spent grabbing lunches, taking calls, and everything else that comes with maintaining them. As a result, I feel like I have so much more freedom. So much more opportunity to invest into areas I'm truly excited about. I want to be clear that it's nothing personal at all. All of those acquaintances are great people, but I just don't have the emotional energy to invest in that many people. And that's okay. It's hard to hold on to that truth sometimes, though. It's so easy to get lost in the errant guilt that comes from feeling like I'm letting someone down — even though I'm truly not.

As a result of editing my life, I do less "things" with less people, but I am fully present and have the energy to give my full self, which is so much better than giving a fraction of myself as I try to survive an endless life of obligation. And because my life is more full of things I'm passionate about and people I deeply care about, who challenge me to be the best I can be, I am infinitely more happy and my creativity is flowing freer than it ever has.

Creativity and happiness require space — they require freedom.

Living a life of intention, of impact, of creativity, requires the best of us we can give. And the only way we can ever hope to do this is to love ourselves enough to say no.

Of all the things I've been able to edit from my life recently, I think the single decision that has created the most freedom in my life is one I made over four years ago. I edited television from my life. Seriously. I canceled my cable subscription, sold my television, and never looked back.

When I first tell people I don't own a television, they're shocked. They can't even begin to imagine parting with their own, but doing so has been one of the most liberating decisions I've ever made — and I have the numbers to prove it.

Did you know that the average American watches 34 hours of live television per week — plus another three to six hours watching taped content? This means that, all told, as a country we watch an average of more than 37 hours of video programming every week.[4]

That stat is incredible to me.

Especially when you consider that we are only awake for about 112 hours per week (16 hours per day). Watching television for 37 hours per week means we essentially have a second full-time job (assuming you already have a full-time job). This means we are wasting almost one third of our waking lives watching non-constructive or just plain mind-numbing media. Yes some of it can be incredibly entertaining or educational, but the truth is most of it is simply designed to bleed hours out of our days and nights, out of our lives, so that networks can serve us an increasing amount of advertising.

To think that with one decision, I've essentially created a full-time-job's worth of free time in my life, is amazing — time I'm now free to use for anything my heart desires. It's time I now spend reading, writing, designing, playing music, playing sports, meeting with friends, or enjoying life with my wife.

I will concede that my wife and I do have Hulu and Netflix accounts so that we can keep up with a few of our favorite shows and watch the occasional movie, but I can say definitively that, on average, I watch no more than three or four hours of programming or movies per week. This means I'm spending about 90% less time blankly staring at a screen than the average person in this country; which creates more than 33 hours of freedom in my life — every single week.

And the impact that extra freedom has had on my life has been substantial.

Yes, the initial separation anxiety existed for a week or

two, and resurfaces every April when I have to get creative about finding a place to watch the Masters golf tournament. But aside from a couple times a year my TV-less life is amazing — because those 33-plus hours a week are now filled with what and those I love.

Space can be such a beautiful thing, if we can find it in ourselves to create it.

I dare you to try it. You won't be disappointed.

BROKEN PARADIGMS

Creating freedom in life, the freedom necessary to create deeply, really involves two factors: freedom of *time* (which I just touched on a bit) and freedom of *mind*.

When I say mind, I'm referring to the paradigms (ways of thinking) that have been pressed on our minds and hearts since the day we were born. Paradigms like religion, education, career, achievement, relationships, entitlement, to name a few. Most of these paradigms stem from everything that comes to mind when we think of the American Dream. Go to church every Sunday. Get good grades in school. Go to a prestigious university. Rack up $100,000 (or more) in student loans. Rack up $10,000 more traveling around Europe. Get a good job. Climb the corporate ladder. Marry a pretty girl. Climb the corporate ladder some more. Rack up another $100,000 (or more) in graduate student loans. Buy a house. Have a kid. On and on and on. Oh, and, somewhere in there, figure out a way to pay back all that debt, while trying to pay for the ever-bigger lifestyle society convinces you to believe you need.

I want to be clear, it's not that any of the facets of the American Dream are necessarily bad in and of themselves (though I will say student loan debt has essentially crippled my entire generation), but the American Dream is a perfect example of our world's overwhelming tendency to hand us a prescription for our lives and beliefs without any regard for what God actually desires for our lives.

At least that's what happened to me.

I bought into this "dream" at an early age. Despite the murmurs deep inside my soul, I pressed on like the good son I was; achieving anything I could achieve, excelling at everything I did, through both natural ability and sheer force of will. At every stage of the game, by all accounts, I was a winner. Junior High and High school Valedictorian? Check. All-League, Varsity athlete? Check. Full ride academic scholarship? Check. Engineering degree from a prestigious university? Check. High-paying job in a buzzing city? Check. Nice car? Check. Pretty Girl? Check. More promotions and cash? Check. Unhappiness? Check...Wait what?

Yes, unhappiness. Insanely deep unhappiness. Want to jump off a cliff unhappy.

Yeah, that kind.

Two years out of college and I found myself so unhappy

with life all I could think about was pulling the plug on everything. I had achieved everything my mind and the world wanted, yet I failed to obtain one single thing my soul actually cared about. My life, up to that point, had been so consumed with everything everyone told me I should be consumed by, I couldn't even tell you what it was my soul was so desperate for. All I knew was I didn't have it.

So I walked away.

From everything.

I quit my job (and didn't look for a new one). I finally let go of the girl (as I mentioned the relationship had exploded a couple months prior, but I was still holding on for some reason I still don't understand). I put the frame that enshrined my degree in a box. I moved out of my two-bedroom flat and rented a room in a stranger's house I found on Craigslist (no more job = no more money for a house). My new room was so tiny I was forced to get rid of all my furniture. All that survived the liquidation was my guitars, golf clubs, books, and a queen-size AeroBed.

I ended up sleeping on that air mattress for over six months. When the day came for me to move on (due to my empty bank account), my entire life fit into my car, bed included. When I was packing, my roommates looked at me with this confused look on their faces and asked, "Where the heck did your bed go?" Without skipping a beat I said, "Oh, it's in the trunk!" They all thought I'd been sleeping on a real mattress. I guess that down comforter was worth the money after all. At least it helped prop up the veneer that my life wasn't sliding as hard as it really was. With my life packed comfortably in my four-door sedan, I turned the corner, left the Las Vegas desert in my rear view, and headed north to California.

But the sliding wasn't done. Even though I had no possessions to speak of left, I still had my car. At least for a bit. It's funny how much of our identities can attach themselves to a few panels of sheet metal with an engine inside. Nevertheless, God saw it fit to remove that from my grasp, too. It was serving too well as a prop for my ego. My car was the last piece of my external identity I had left. But with no income, no savings left, and debt piling up, it wasn't long before I was finally forced to sell it. And when I did, the last ounce of dignity I had left drove away in the hands of some teenage girl and her loving parents. Ironically, she wasn't much different than me seven years earlier.

As my now-former car turned the corner in the parking lot out of view, I looked into my own eyes in the rear view mirror and my soul finally hit rock bottom. I was twenty-three, unemployed, living with my parents, and sitting in the driver seat of a 1999 Volkswagen Jetta that was such a beater I drove in constant fear that it might explode. And by beater, I mean it in its fullest form. Seriously, the thing *barely* made it home the day I bought it. The $2200 I paid for it was pretty much all I had to my name, so you can imagine the nausea that ensued twenty minutes into the trip home as it began throwing up water like one of those seltzer volcanoes you make in elementary school. I guess that's what you get when you buy a used car with a flashing check engine light from a couple shady kids in the heart of Oakland.

I know all of our rock bottoms look different, but this was surely one for me. I was broke both worldly and spiritually, without the slightest clue how to stop the spinning.

Piece by piece I was forced to surrender everything I had accumulated. Everything for which I had strived. Everything for which I had given up myself. Everything the world had convinced me I needed. God was more than obliging to remove the lingering pieces I was holding onto for dear life. In the end, the Jetta only lasted a few months before the engine finally did blow up on the freeway. As if my ego wasn't broken enough, I had to resort to borrowing one of my parents' cars for the next year. Despite looking like a football, at least the 1999 Chrysler had leather seats and a working stereo to dampen the blow of being a complete-and-utter dependent at age twenty-four.

I won't lie, those last pieces of my artificial identify hurt the most to lose. Descending the first ninety-nine percent of the way is relatively easy in comparison to the last one percent. The last one percent is what crushes you. Nothing breaks you open more, and cuts deeper, than losing the last of what we have left. That last one percent can be anything. For me, it was my nice car. It was the only thing I had left that I could use to project to everyone else that I was still "successful." It's in losing that last piece of who you are that God shoves you into the abyss, where the only way to survive is to cling to Him for dear life.

And that's the point.

God is after nothing less than our total and utter dependence on Him for our very existence. And the only way for that to happen is for us to reach what I call Ground Zero (more on this in a bit).

What was most interesting was that having to let go of something external forced me to release myself from the mental paradigm that was associated with it. I didn't realize it then, but everything external I had achieved for myself was attached to, and a result of, a belief, a value, I held.

I wasn't a prisoner because of my external self. I was a prisoner of my internal self. A prisoner of my own mind. My own values. My own beliefs. My own paradigms.

My mind had created a world-driven image of my own self. A version of me that couldn't be further from who God had intended me to be, from who my soul wanted so desperately for me to be.

Before I walked away from everything, I couldn't accurately name one thing I was passionate about. It took the first twenty-three years of my life, but the only thing I had truly achieved was the fulfillment of Matthew 16:26:

> *What good will it be for someone to gain the whole world, yet lose their soul? What can anyone give in exchange for their soul?*

Even scarier was the reality that it wasn't, seemingly, a conscious choice, but one subtly and convincingly pitched by an incessant, hell-bent society that took over my soul inch by inch. And worse, in all my brokenness and humanity, I was a willing and eager customer. As a result, my internal and external worlds were filled so fully by the world's version of what I should be passionate about that there wasn't room for any of my real desires.

I was an empty shell.

A shadow of what God had intended me to be.

Just as our days need to be free of time-expensive obligations, our minds and hearts need to be free from poisonous paradigms (and the "things" we fill our lives with as a result), if we're ever to find our true selves and desires.

It takes both external and internal freedom to find ourselves. True creation requires this same freedom because it demands intimacy.

Intimacy with who we truly are.
Intimacy with our souls.
Intimacy with our Creator.

And the only way for us to find room in our lives for freedom, is to let go of everything else.

GROUND ZERO

I know I've touched on this already but I think it's worth unpacking this idea of Ground Zero a bit more. If I were to try to define it further, I would say that Ground Zero is the place where we have completely died unto ourselves. And it's in that death that we find true and limitless freedom. It's the physical, material, and spiritual place where all worldly distractions have been removed. It's the place where our hands and hearts are empty and our egos have nothing external to attach themselves to except our true identity in Christ.

Letting go of, and dying to, ourselves is a process full of deep emotional pain and desperate longing. It shatters our ego and leaves us on the ground in pieces. Yet it is in this void that God, in His infinite mercy and love, gathers up the wreckage and restores our spiritual freedom and divine identities. It is in this freedom and intimacy that we are able to enjoy God's creation and express ourselves through creation of our own without feeding our egos — because in Ground Zero, in our complete realization of our brokenness, our hearts are overwhelmed with humility and gratitude.

I believe we have been given the ability to create because God desires for us join Him in increasing the beauty of the universe through the expression of our divinely-crafted identities. Identities that carry with them an intimate glimpse into the heart of our Creator. If that is true, then taking this purpose one step further leaves us with our ultimate and true purpose: *to express the heart of our Creator through who we are and what we create.*

When we create from Ground Zero, everything we create ultimately expresses the love, mercy, and beauty of our Maker, because, whether we realize it or believe it, at our core is even more than us — it's Him.

Most creative inspiration, it seems, comes from a place of great pain. I think most inspiration comes from this place because often the seasons of greatest pain and struggle are the very same seasons God uses to bring us to Ground Zero. God reveals Himself, and His desires for our lives, in the times of our greatest need. When we are broken. When we've lost it all. When we've turned our backs on everything. When we've given it all away.

It's in those moments of brokenness that God has finally pried open enough space in our lives to show Himself.[5] It's in the darkness that we find light, because in the day we are blinded by the brightness of our own egos. In order for us to find God, our egos must pass away. We must be free. Free from ourselves.

It is in this freedom of spirit that we discover our greatest inspiration, because the seasons of our greatest struggles are often also the stories of our greatest liberations. Pain and joy are two sides of the same coin. And in Ground Zero, both realities coexist in complete unity.

It's the inflection point of the soul.

The collision of light and dark, pain and joy, creates a cosmic friction that sparks the eternal fire deep in our souls, and drives our internal experiences outward in bold explosions of creativity. Divine friction throws sparks on a cosmic scale. It is from this space that we become vessels of our Creator. Ground Zero is the place where our Creator has finally freed our souls and lives enough to use us.

We must create from this place. It's where we are most aware of ourselves, the world around us, and our Creator. It's where our emotions and desires are the most lucid, our convictions most raw, and the divine friction the most violent.

It's this place of friction, the process of friction, that God uses to create the sparks of creativity. Sparks that shower the world every day with glimpses of God's infinite love for us, and point to the greater story of redemption God is ever-pressing on our hearts.

INSPIRATION IS FLEETING

Freedom is the crux of the entire existence of a creator. It is the keystone. If creation is instinctive, we need the freedom, the ability, to respond. Our creativity lives and dies at the hands of our ability to respond in the moment to inspiration because moments of creative inspiration are always fleeting. You have to embrace them when they present themselves, else we risk losing them forever. Putting inspiration on hold is essentially the same as killing it completely. Sometimes it's possible to resurrect a resemblance of the original urge, but it will never take the same shape as it would have if you allowed it to express itself fully in the moment. If the goal of our lives is to be vessels of God's will, then we must be free and open to respond to His desires in the moment He desires to fulfill them through us.

This is why creating freedom in our lives is so important.

Case in point, it's past 1 a.m. as I'm writing this. I'm completely exhausted, but I have this incredibly strong creative urge at the moment, and after trying to shove it to the background, I'm now typing away on my laptop. I'm not sure of the purpose, but I'm trusting in the desire. It started a couple minutes ago. A single thought came into my head. I grabbed my laptop and wrote it down. *A reminder for tomorrow*, I told myself. A couple minutes later, another thought. *I'll make a mental note*, I told myself as I rolled over in bed too tired to open my computer a second time. Thirty seconds of internal deliberation later, I'm now typing away and, in a way I didn't associate initially, the two thoughts are now weaving themselves together in this dialogue. (The first thought was around how creation is humbling because it forces us to open ourselves and intimately share a glimpse of who we are with the world. The second thought was around this idea that creative inspiration is always fleeting and we have to trust in the impulses in the moments they present themselves - else we risk losing them forever.)

Why couldn't I let it go? Something deep within me is telling me this is important. Do I understand why? No. Do I know how this is going to be important? Again, no. So why, then, am I pressing on and writing all of this down? I believe in the guidance God provides us through our desires, our inspirations. I'm trusting that my choice to be a conduit for what He has planted in me (whatever that may be) will bring something positive to the world, and His kingdom — be it in an external manifestation (like this book), or simply in my own internal, personal preparation for what lies ahead. From my own story, I can attest that our understanding of God's method of provision is not a prerequisite in God's leadership. In fact, I believe that in order for us to be able to fully trust in His leadership, we can't understand. We must release ourselves from the desire to know as His intention for our lives is one built on intimate faith and reliance on Him. He provides for us one step at a time, and, usually, He only provides the next step when we take the step before.

God always knows exactly where we are going, but God doesn't build runways.

Or if He does, He surely doesn't let us see them.

We never know when inspiration will present itself, or if it will result in anything of purpose (that we can perceive). Yet this trusting of our divine instincts is another key perspective when we think about this idea of freedom. Without trust in our Creator, trust in the desires He's written on our hearts, and trust in what flows from Him and through us, we can never create freely and nakedly.

This type of trust isn't trivial. Or easy to give. It's like having to trust someone to lead you across a six-lane freeway blindfolded during rush hour. It's a real-life game of Frogger. We don't understand all the moving parts. We don't know where we're going, or even where our foot is going to land the next time we take a step. Yet it's in this trust, in our faith, that we find the third and most expansive freedom of all — spiritual freedom. (Remember, we've previously discussed time, which is material freedom, and breaking free of worldly paradigms, which is mental freedom)

Trust, though, is always in a tug-of-war with fear. In the life of a creator, fear is the paramount counter-emotion to our desire to create. Acts of creation require that we open ourselves, our hearts, to the world. In that openness exists undeniable, and often overwhelming, vulnerability. In our openness, we expose ourselves to the possibilities of hurt, criticism, silence, violence, protest, apathy, and embarrassment. But we can't lose site of the reality that, in that same moment, we also open ourselves to growth, progress, purpose — fulfillment. In the risk there is reward. But we have to believe it wholeheartedly because we don't have the luxury of knowing what the response to our creation will be. As humans, we must create out of blind faith.

And it's terrifying.

Yet it is in this struggle between our vulnerability and need to create, between our fear and need to trust, that we discover humility. It's in this moment of nakedness that we come to understand — it's in this place of humility that we find freedom. It is a divine paradox. In our submission we become free. Maybe that is what Luke meant in his gospel when he wrote:

> Whoever tries to keep their lives will lose it, and whoever loses his life will preserve it.[6]

Creation is as much about freedom as it is about trust. True creation only exists when we create from our Ground Zero. Only when we create from this place of vulnerability and humility, can we begin to discover what God is trying to create through us.[7]

THROWING UP INSPIRATION

Well, it's been quite a while since I've been able to quiet my soul to the point where it's able to write. Friction in life is an insurmountable barrier to the tranquility of mind writing requires. And I've been far, far away from that place.

They always say the calm comes after the storm. I wouldn't go as far to say I'm calm, but it's definitely been stormy lately.

It's been quite a challenging time for me creatively, as a result of the chaos. I find it interesting that chaos, in retrospect, can be an incredible source of creative inspiration. Yet attempting to create in the midst of it is almost fruitless. It might even be more accurately described as frustrating — because everything in you wants your soul to quiet itself so the creativity inside you can blossom at its own pace. Yet life has a way of cornering us into throwing up our inspiration in short, frantic spurts. Leaving us feeling exposed and empty — violated.

Frantic and fragmented, life perverts our creativity. It fragments our inspiration as if it were shattering a porcelain vase on the ground. A vase that you can't put back together.

Creativity is an instinct. But it must be chosen. It must be channeled. Creativity is a lot like a flower. It must be cultivated, cared for — loved, because it can just as easily be perverted, prostituted, ignored, squelched, silenced — neglected.

Creativity is the central experience of the human heart because it is the core of our identity, our being. As a result, just as we must emphatically "guard our hearts," as one of my favorite authors John Eldredge is oft to say, we must uncompromisingly guard our creativity. I've been doing a poor job of this lately. I can feel the damage in my chest. I can feel the ever-present frustration hardening my heart.

The world, and Satan, are constantly trying to shut our hearts down. And they are phenomenal at it. Just think about this for a minute: How many kids spend great amounts of time drawing? Every single one. How many adults spend great amounts of time drawing? Almost none. It's the same soul, but with one big difference: When we're young, our hearts are open, and creativity flourishes. Creativity literally explodes from within us with an intensity of imagination few of us can retain into our double-digit years. But, as the years pile on our hearts, our hearts sink into the confinement of an obligation-filled existence that seldom resembles the freeing and expressive life we were created to live.

Creativity is the symptom of a heart that is overwhelmingly alive.

No heart, no creativity. No creativity, no heart.

For me, writing requires the greatest stillness of heart of all the creative mediums I express myself through. I feel the most connected to myself, my creativity, and my Creator, in these moments that I feel inspired to write. In this moment, I am just now realizing how important it is for me to do whatever it takes to keep my heart in a place where it's open to express itself through the written word. I spend most of my time creating in the visual world because I feel like I can "force" visual creativity much more than written (and also because, for better or worse, I've been following the money). But in those moments where my heart pours itself out onto a page, my heart sings. My soul exhales. And I find true peace in the moment, and in myself.

What's interesting is that, to this point in my life, it has been my visual creativity that has most compensated me in the world's eyes (aka financially). Yet personally, it has been the time I've spent expressing myself through the written word that has most impacted my spiritual and external lives. The written word (I also include writing music in this as music is the art of giving poetry a voice) is essential to who I am. And I've never fully understood this until this moment. And now I'm beginning to realize just how absent writing has been in different periods of my life. I can firmly say that most periods of my life that I've felt spiritually disconnected were also periods of life where I was unable to find enough stillness in my heart to write.

Interesting.

After writing, I would say tactile, physical, by-hand activities open up my heart in ways visual activities can never compare. It actually wasn't until that day I spent at IDEO a couple months ago that my heart was re-awakened to its love for building physical things. Since that day, I've begun a project to design and create a messenger bag entirely by myself. It has been such a wonderfully creative experience for me. I feel like I've been awakened to this huge part of me that has been locked away dormant for the past fifteen years. Creative loves of mine that had been completely forgotten have exploded back into the forefront of my mind. Loves I'd lost before I left middle school. And now my creativity is pouring through this tactile, three-dimensional lens. I'm not sure what has my heart more excited: the rediscovery of a lost part of my identity, or all that is flowing out of me as a result of this spiritual and creative restoration.

Given all this, what's interesting is that, right now, I'm actually making my living by using my third-most spiritual form of creativity. Which means I'm living a large portion of my life operating two "levels" away from my spiritual core. I am not, by any means, disgruntled. Yet I sense my heart slowly leading me in the direction of the other two mediums. And the more I understand my heart and rediscover areas I've lost, the more I'm coming to trust that my natural instincts will guide me in that direction. And it's my hope that some day I will be able to transition into a more tactile endeavor, en route to a place in my life where I will be able to devote my heart freely to writing.

It is not to say that I won't be spending time in all three areas concurrently, but that the three will crescendo in order, in terms of the amount of time I'm able to spend in them, and the impact they'll have on my own heart and the hearts of others. In a worldly sense, the progression seems obvious as the weight of words are exponentially tied to the preceding actions of the person who writes them. So for now, I'm trying to focus on the actions while chronicling my heart's creative journey; in hopes that the words might help, in some miniscule way, guide others to a similar rediscovery of their identity and the pieces of their hearts that have long slipped away.

All the clues are hidden in our innocence, in our freedom — in our youth. We are all creative in millions of different ways. The journey is about discovering which of those amplifies our heart's voice the most. All of us have (at the very least) that "one thing." That one medium of creativity that seems to truly unite us with our divine identity. It's in those moments of intimacy with our true selves that we also discover what our souls are crying out for the most — unparalleled intimacy with our loving Creator.

IF YOU DON'T LOVE IT, YOU WILL FAIL.

I just watched an interview with Steve Jobs where he was talking about the need to love what you were doing.[8] In short, he said love for your mission was critical because without such a deep passion, you'll never be able to endure through all the intense trials life brings.

But the magically enticing side of the struggle is how undeniable the impact on the world a person can create when they actually stumble into what it is they truly love. Steve Jobs found what he loved to do. So did Einstein, Picasso, Hemingway, Shakespeare, my friend Jena who's wanted to be a nurse since she was ten, and some of my coworkers who are sold out on corporate life.

These people live and breathe their passions. And people who live out of their spiritual passions change the world.

And not in some trivial nudging of the needle, but in a disruptive, revolutionary sort of way. So profound, the world can't help but take note.

We all want to experience life from that depth of connection with ourselves, with our Creator. But the reality is, it's a tough, tough search. Our hell-bent world is determined to keep us separated from our true selves and occupied by distraction. We concede ourselves for jobs, money, friends, relationships, prestige, accolades, achievement, acceptance, greed, and obligations. We abandon ourselves for the life that's constantly being sold to us every time we pick up a newspaper, turn on the TV or radio, or listen to some company CEO spin "Kool-Aid" to his troops.

We get so consumed by the life the world is selling that we completely forget about the life Jesus is constantly trying to *give* us: a passion-centered, free-spirited life, where we live life from our spiritual identity in Him and the love He has for us.

For Free.

No spin selling required.

Yet I'm still searching because the sad reality is, I don't look to Jesus very often for the answer to the most fundamental question in my life: "Who am I?" I constantly look to the world for the answer to that question, and all I get in return is the world's errant opinion of who it wants me to be.

It seems so simple when you think about it. If I want so

badly to know who I am, shouldn't my Creator be the first place I turn? I mean, after all, He created me in His own image.

But I forget.

We all forget.

And it's not until we find our hands full of all the things the world wants us to hold dear that we realize our souls have died somewhere along the way. From there, there are two roads: keep collecting as our soul withers, or choose Jesus and let everything fall.

One thing I am grateful for is that as good as I am at accumulating a worldly identity, God is equally as good at stripping it away. He screams at us through our hearts — if we choose to hear His voice. I've dropped so many seemingly "good" things at the surprise of everyone around me, and every time it feels so freeing. We all struggle with picking up a worldly life, but the people who ultimately discover their true passions are masters at putting that worldly life back down when the two don't match. You have to listen to your heart. Your heart is the voice of your divinely designed identity — of God.

Happiness is only found when we choose God and the life He designed us to live.

I need to get better at leaning on Jesus. We're all good at picking things up, but Jesus makes us good at putting them down. And in time, we learn to only pick up what is truly important. We know, because we know who we are.

Because we went to the only person in the universe who can tell us: our Creator.

FOUR

ALL THINGS NEW

"And so long as you haven't experienced this: to die and so to grow, you are only a troubled guest on the dark earth."

—Johan Wolfgang von Goethe

HERE GOES NOTHING

I've been really conflicted these past few weeks. My heart has been turning over on itself as I've deliberated whether or not to include the section you're about to read. I've done everything I can do to remove it, but there's something in my heart that won't let me hit the delete button. I've tried to re-write it, I've tried to soften the tone, but for some reason the paragraphs won't budge.

To be honest, I'm terrified by the words that you are about to read. But despite my efforts to side step the voice in my heart, I can't deny the reality that these words may be the most honest of them all. If true creation demands full exposure and vulnerability, this most certainly will be the crescendo for me.

In the face of how terrifying it feels to share what follows, I have come too far to not leave everything on the table. I need to find the courage to pour my heart out one more time, and pray for God's infinite wisdom and grace along the way.

Before I begin, I want you to know I say all this with a loving, searching, longing heart — a heart empty of malice or condemnation, but a heart captivated by the excitement for a God whose story is ever unfolding.

Here goes nothing.

A CONFESSION

I have a confession.

Something I've spent my entire life carrying around inside because I've been too scared to share it with anyone. I've even spent the majority of this book holding it in, but my heart wants so desperately to come clean. So as much as it terrifies me to say this, I'm just going to lay it out there.

I really struggle with church.

Seriously. I *really* struggle with it. So much so, that in all honesty, I might actually even resent it at this point. There's something about the entire church charade that has become almost revolting to me.

I should clarify, when I say "church," I'm referring to the standard, institutionalized, modern-day version of the local church that we are all familiar with as Americans. I'm talking about the *business* that church has become, *not* the people it's comprised of. For me, the church experience, which according to most everyone, is supposed to be this rewarding, God-filled experience that draws me deeper and closer to my Creator, has felt more akin to an expensive, empty, hamster wheel of rituals, programs, services — obligations. And because all these things are being sold as the way to spiritual intimacy with God, I've spent my entire life feeling guilty that all it's ever seemed to feel like for me was agony. The agony a square peg must feel like when someone's trying to shove it incessantly into a round hole.

Over time, the frustration and discontent made me believe

there was something wrong with me. I would question myself constantly.

Why am I so disenchanted?

Why do I feel emptier and further from God the more I try to connect myself with the church?

I spent years (decades, really) struggling through the same cycle: nine months of deep consistent involvement, where I would give my time, attendance, and resources to all the events, services, and projects the church offered, only to find myself at the end so discouraged, frustrated, tired — empty, from the whole charade that I would need to take a "church fast" (as I've come to call it) for three to four months to allow my soul to recover.

I thought this was normal.

Or at least in the sense that it's normal for *me* to be struggling in this area of "church." Every fast served as further confirmation that I hadn't "grown" in my walk enough to feel fulfilled by all of "God's work" I'd been taking part in.

I've spent twenty-seven years now living like this: carrying the guilt of believing something was deeply wrong with my soul, burying frustration, watching others seemingly blossom as they jumped through all the hoops — while I bounced from church to church searching for something that would quiet the gag reflex in my soul, or searching for no church at all because I'd given up hope for ever finding something that would bring resolution to my starving soul.

Yet, amidst all the struggle, deep down, I just couldn't come to grips with the idea that my burning desire to connect with God, and my inability to achieve it through all the "ways" I'd been taught to pursue Him, were the result of some deep flaw within my soul. Because, despite my frustration with the church, I absolutely love God with all my heart and want nothing more than to grow closer in intimacy with Him and with others who desire the same.

Something deep within me recently began to manifest itself, a small flicker of a voice, a spark, that asked a simple, yet monumental question:

What if it's not you that's broken; what if it's the paradigm?

The question made me pause, as I realized my entire perspective on what a quote-un-quote spiritual life looked like was defined through the lens of what others had told me was right. I realized that instead of spending time truly searching to understand what God desires for my life, our lives, I'd simply taken the modern-day church's word for it.

And as I pressed deeper into that question, it didn't take long for the paradigm I'd been given to completely unravel.

STEPPING BACK

My wife and I have lived in San Francisco for almost two years now. Not soon after we moved, we got plugged into a young church plant here in the city. When we joined, the group was about a dozen people and we met in the living room of our pastor's house. We met this way for almost seven months. The numbers of people fluctuated some, but the numbers ultimately never grew. And for those seven months, that was entirely okay. We loved how the smaller scale helped foster intimacy and gave us the opportunity to truly get to know one another and build real relationships. Everything we were as a community seemed to resonate with all the New Testament stories that tell of early Christians gathering in small numbers and seeking to live life intimately with one another.

In a word, everything felt right.

Yet, despite all this, at the end of those seven months, the pastor (and I'm sure the church planting organization that was supporting him) decided we needed to "go public," or in the Christian community's eyes, "become a real church." At first I couldn't understand why would we do this in the face of zero growth, zero need for more space, and, in all honesty, zero real desire as a group to be anything more than what we already were. But as our conversations and plans progressed, I realized we were doing this because in the world's eyes, at least in this country, in this century, twelve people meeting in a living room isn't considered "church." To be a "real church" today, you need a building, you need to preach an hour-long sermon, you need to have a band play for thirty minutes, you need coffee, daycare, a sound system — aka you need a Sunday "show." With the show in place, you then need to start collecting tithes to pay for all of the above plus the pastor's salary, as now he must be supported full-time because someone needs to manage the weekly production of this newly minted "church." And lastly, the members of the "congregation" must now spend the majority of their Sundays helping to put on this "service."

As time accelerated us towards the launch, it became increasingly difficult to make sense of what was happening. Not really understanding the weight of the decisions we were making, and, honestly, driven by a fear of being left behind, my wife and I jumped in with both feet and gave our blessing. We gave our time and talents as best we could and even assumed leadership positions over several key functions. But despite our earnest efforts to support our church's metamorphosis, something in my soul revolted. In the pressure of the moment, I couldn't get my heart around the specifics, but everything about what we were doing tasted wrong.

It was like a spiritual gag reflex.

As the first week rolled into the second, I tried to find resolution with our decisions, but I couldn't escape the undeniable feeling that there was something wrong with twelve people running around like crazy all week trying to prepare a weekend "service" for the very same twelve people to attend. There was also something especially wrong with passing around an offering plate to those same twelve people to pay for the "show," the building, and the equipment — all so the pastor could have a "platform" to preach.

It just seemed completely errant to me.

Especially when the previous weekend's gathering in his

living room was entirely free. A couple weeks into the new "endeavor," completely overwhelmed by what was transpiring and searching for clarity, I asked the pastor what was driving his decision to step out like this. His response was, "This small group is great, but we can't just do this forever...I can't really preach from my living room."

I then asked him, "Why are we taking on the burden of a larger space when we aren't even fully using the space we have here in your living room? Many of the communities of believers I know of expand their space out of need."

He replied, "It's not good to get locked into a particular kind of model for a church...Sometimes if things aren't growing you need to *force* it."

Force it?

My soul threw up.

I was expecting the classic, "I've been in a lot of prayer about this and I really feel God leading us in this direction."

Instead, I got the antithesis.

Now I'm not sure if he miscommunicated the true posture of his heart or if his response came through a rare glimpse of transparency, but we left the church the next week. It was three weeks after the "launch." The church only kept its doors open for a few months before shutting down. Two years of preparation and tens of thousands of dollars of seed money later, the story ended before it ever truly began. Another "church" chewed up and spit out by this unforgiving city, I guess.

At least that's the story the statistics will tell.

As I watched everything fall apart, I was left with a heart full of questions and void of answers.

What exactly did the pastor feel so strongly he needed to force?

Where was all that pressure coming from?

How could it feel so wrong, and ultimately end so badly, when all the things we did were all the things the world believes it means to be a church in our society?

Why did we all eagerly go along with it?

Where was God?

When all we have to hold onto is rhetorical questions, I know our only real choice is to leave it in God's hands and trust that He's ever making good with our collective experiences. But, I must admit, as much as my heart knows this to be true, I'm finding it impossible to reconcile the amount of external pressure we were all under to "launch" our church. It was absolutely bigger than the sum of us. In hindsight, I don't think we ever really stood a chance. Our pastor's spiritual strength and our collective desires to make disciples for Jesus were completely dwarfed by the immensity of what we *had* to be in the broader community's eyes.

That's why this story isn't really about us, our pastor, or our church — it's a story about expectations.

I think it's worth emphasizing further that I don't doubt for a moment our pastor's love for Christ and the true calling God placed on his heart to lead people to relationship with Jesus. He's a phenomenal teacher and there's no doubt that God called him to this city. And for answering that call, he is truly courageous. I hope to be half the man of God he is someday. To think of the sacrifices he and his family made to start a church in the most unchurched city in America, to share their love of Jesus with all of us, is truly humbling. His devotion and love for God are a constant reminder of just how far I have yet to go.

I decided to share our story because I think our story is illustrative of the overbearing and misplaced expectations that millions of pastors and communities around the world are struggling to fulfill every day.

In an effort to deconstruct the circumstances that surrounded our collapse, I've spent the last year trying to get to the heart of that pressure.

In the wake of all that's happened in my life in the area of church, and the scars all of it has left on my heart, I've come to realize that it's impossible for me to make sense of my life's collective experiences with church because I've spent my entire life simply accepting everything the world has taught me about church and absolutely zero time seeking to understand what God and Jesus *actually* say about church.

Desperate to find solace, I've spent the past few months in study and in prayer, seeking to better understand the heart of what Jesus commissioned in Acts some two thousand years ago, and how I — how all of us, really — fit into that story.[1]

As a result of my inquisition, I've come to the conclusion that the pressure is the result of this collective paradigm, this belief, we all hold in our society about what "church" actually is.

The pressure is the *model.*

And the model is a product of what we've been told our entire lives about what the Bible (the Book of Acts in particular) *supposedly* says about church.

I say "supposedly" because I was astonished to discover most of it *isn't* true.

EKKLESIA

The first eye-opening truth I discovered came from a desire to understand what the word "church" even means. We use the term in such an array of ways these days that it's hard to keep sight of what the Bible's actual definition is.

Today the word "church" can mean anything from a building, to a congregation, to a functioning corporation, to outreach, to a small group — to whatever really. I don't know if you've noticed this or not, but we love to quote Ephesians 5:25 these days and say "God loves the church." And what I find most interesting is, we love to quote the verse in defense of any and every spin of the word our human hands desire to create. Ephesians 5:25 is typically the companion verse every pastor quotes as they teach through Acts in order to skim through the topic of how exactly our "contextualized and relevant" church syncs up with the image that's painted in the text.

It seems that in our culture and society, if we can somehow put something underneath, or associate it with, some variation of the word "church," then we can immediately cover and justify it by saying, "God loves the church." And because no one wants to contest something "God loves," we agree and put our hearts, time, and dollars behind the mission.

Ephesians 5:25 is the ultimate validation.

But is our interpretation of it true?

Is God's definition of church and *our* definition of church the same?

Something about it doesn't feel right. I mean, can we really cover every definition of "church" we dream up with the truth of Ephesians?

In God's eyes, in the Bible, what does "church" really mean?

I've been spent countless hours digging into this question. Here's what I've found:

In our English Bible, the Greek word *ekklesia* is translated in most places as "church." The word *ekklesia* is used one hundred and eighteen times in the New Testament. It is translated in English one hundred and fifteen times as "church" and the remaining three times as "assembly."

The word *ekklesia,* as used in the New Testament, is actually a compound of two classical Greek roots: *ek* which means "away from" and *kaleo* which means "to call out." In New Testament times, the word was exclusively used to represent an assembly of people who had been called out of their homes for a particular purpose. It was never used explicitly to refer to a religious meeting or group.[2]

Based on the above, a more accurate translation of *ekklesia* would be, "the called out ones."

Or in a biblical context, the people Jesus has called out, has set aside as His own — His followers.

Not a building, not programs, not sermons, not songs.

People.

When I discovered that the Bible is referring exclusively to "God's people" when it uses the word "church" or *ekklesia,* the truth that "God loves the church" took on an entirely different, and much more profound, meaning. It also made it seem like a bit of a stretch to hear the phrase quoted to defend any institutionalized form of the modern-day "church."

Just because God loves us doesn't always mean He loves

what we do.

I can think of a million things God doesn't love about the decisions I've made and continue to make. Yet wouldn't it seem odd to my friends and family if I started justifying my actions by saying, "God loves me, so it's not right to assess my actions?"

Not to say we do it intentionally, but, to me, it feels as if we're doing something similar.

I want to be clear that my heart in this thought is not to judge, or condemn the hearts of Jesus' followers who make up the modern-day church, as I think we all are earnestly seeking God with honest and heartfelt intentions. But I do want to highlight that using "God loves the church" to justify building a huge campus complex, or to defend huge pastoral salaries or any other facet of the "corporation," is wrong. God loves His people. God wants us to have an intimate relationship with Him.

That's it.

It's truly that simple.

There's some real beauty in the way the New Testament describes the early church. It simply tells the *story* of the early believers. It isn't prescriptive. It isn't definitive. It doesn't specify a step-by-step model as the Old Testament does, full of rules and regulations and laws — religion.

I think if we can learn anything from the Old Testament it's that humans are more than capable of perverting a divine recipe for life. Instead, God, through Jesus, did something beautiful and completely subversive.

He abolished religion entirely and set us free.

He set us free so that we could chase Him, seek Him, love Him, and express His love for us to others through the infinite number of ways He moves in us. If the New Testament teaches us anything, it's that models should be held loosely at best, if not cast away entirely.

Models are built on religion. A Jesus-led life is built on faith.

And because God is inviting us into a faith-led life, God doesn't care about methods. Reconciling ourselves to God through Jesus is all that matters.

I think it's worth repeating. Jesus did not come to establish a new religion, but to eliminate religion entirely.[3]

This revelation has shown me that it's okay to feel the way I do. It doesn't mean that others don't or won't find incredible fulfillment being a part of more traditional congregations. If you do, that's wonderful and I'm thrilled that you're growing in relationship with God and other believers through that. But if you're not, it's okay, and biblical, to seek intimacy with God and community with other believers in whatever manners God calls you to — and to do it *guilt free.*

There are no models.

Only the direct relationship we have with our Creator and

the relationships we have with each other matter.

Everything else is religion.

WE WANT ATTENDEES, JESUS WANTS DISCIPLES.

As we've discussed, sparks come from intense focus, pressure — friction. Jesus was the epitome of focus. With an entire universe to save, He picked twelve ordinary people and poured the vast majority of His energy into just those twelve.

Seriously, twelve people. That's it. Crazy, right? It's so counter intuitive to the age of mega-churches that we're living in today, it will spin your mind in knots.

It's easy for us to lose sight of this reality in today's culture, but the truth is this:

Jesus of Nazareth is the most successful mini-church pastor of all time.

Yet today we have a not-so-subtle difference in aim: we only want to start mega-churches.

Jesus starts a mini-church, and somewhere along the way we, His *followers*, decide that mega-churches are somehow a better way.

It's an interesting discrepancy. I'm not fully privy to how the story unfolded to get us to where we are today, but it really does seem errant when you take a step back from it. Our current obsession with crowds seems like a complete lack of focus.

If you were to ask an average person what they would do to grow a business, a product, a church, most would answer with things like market online, advertise in magazines, run promotions and contests, pass out fliers with cookies, set up social media accounts, grab a bull horn and head downtown — aka broadcast the message to as many people as possible, across as many mediums as possible, as loudly as possible.

Yet Jesus gives us the exact opposite answer. Jesus spent the first thirty years of His life essentially out of the spotlight. He then spent the next three years focusing the vast majority of His time, effort, care, and love into His twelve disciples. He did spend time with the broader community at large and spoke to large crowds, but it was seemingly in moderation. It definitely wasn't the central focus of His efforts. And even when He did, His parting request to the masses wasn't, "Tell everyone you can." No, instead He says, "Do not tell anyone what you have seen."[4]

Don't tell? Really?

This makes absolutely no sense to us. If you were sent to save the entirety of the human race, all of creation, wouldn't you want to come out with bullhorns blaring? I know I would. And it's exactly what we have done. We've transformed church into weekly rock concerts that we host in extravagant auditoriums with professional sound and video production, and complemented it all with masterful and captivating monologues — all by paid professionals.

We require professionals because, in our culture, the product matters. And maybe that's the deeper issue. We've turned the church into a sea of corporations and the Gospel of Jesus into a product we must sell better than the other team three blocks away. It's the only way to keep our multi-million dollar campus' lights running and the six-figure pastoral salary checks clearing.

Corporations cost a lot of money to maintain and even more to build, which means, as Christians, we have a lot of selling to do. It's no wonder American Christianity has become what it is today. We are so consumed by the struggle to win everybody's attention that we've lost sight of the truth that:

Our God-given mission is to win hearts through intimacy and focus.

But it's hard to focus on winning hearts when we've grouped ourselves into individual teams. Because in order for our corporations (churches) to survive, we have to market ourselves better than the other teams (churches). We have to provide better music and media (worship), or better teaching (pastors), or a better stadium (auditorium/ campus), or better benefits (classes, daycare, coffee, food, parking, comfortable seats). When you look at what we call church today in this way, it starts to sound more and more like the NFL, MLB, or NBA.

We've turned church into a pro sport.

So much so that pastor's commonly refer to their annual programs in terms of "ministry seasons." As church-goers (the non-professionals), our faith has often been diluted to nothing more than weighing between which "team" we want to play for. We've turned church selection in this country into nothing more than glorified, bandwagon free-agency. All we have to do is pick the "team" that's offering the best "package." Once we sign with a "team," all we have to do is give our "biblical" obligation of money (tithe — more on this later), and volunteer a little bit to help keep the corporation afloat. In return, we get free baby sitting, snacks, entertainment, classes — oh, and yeah, I almost forgot, salvation.

Fueled by our desperate need for relevance, in an increasingly distracted world, the extrapolation feels out of control.

Our Sundays have become larger than life because we keep trying to turn church "up to eleven."[5]

Our efforts to outpace one another have intensified to the point where I'm left struggling to connect the simplicity of the Acts story with that of the highly produced Christian life we're being offered — and eagerly consuming.

It's a gap I'm having a hard time reconciling, but I think it boils down to this:

We want attendees, Jesus wants disciples.

Because of this need to "feed the machine," I believe it has led us, as believers, to lose sight of the life Christ exemplified for us: a life consumed by communion, intimacy, and discipleship — focus. It's so counter to what we know of church today that it almost seems too simple.

The truth that Jesus was *only* interested in gaining disciples is so counterintuitive to everything I know church to be that trying to absorb it immediately causes my mind to start running in the opposite direction:

But aren't we supposed to grow our church?
How are we going to best broadcast our message on Facebook and Twitter?
If we're going to spread the Good News, we're going to need to get structured, get organized, and we're going to need to build a place for all of us to gather.
Then, of course, we're going to have to give people an exciting reason to come by hiring top-notch talent!

But if we ground our hearts in Jesus' example and rest in it's power, our minds have to stop. We have to stop, because Jesus does *none* of that. He simply selects twelve *ordinary* men, and pours everything He has into them. He did life with them. He taught them by walking the streets, living life together, and working through all that the world brought their way. All the while, telling all whom He met along the way to *not* spread the word to others.

Jesus chose less because in less, we have the opportunity to focus our time, energy, and resources on what truly matters. Focus is what creates true, deep, resounding, transcendent impact, because focus creates friction. And in that place of deep and focused friction of the soul, sparks are born.

Sparks start fires.

Sparks start revolutions.

Or in the case of Jesus, twelve sparks ignited the global church. The church that is still on fire over two thousand years later.

Why?

Because Jesus' mission wasn't to build mega-churches. Jesus' mission was to save humanity by igniting the hearts of twelve men who would in turn, in His likeness, set the world ablaze — one heart at a time.

GIVING BY AUTO-DEPOSIT

Another interesting thing I've realized is that giving in the New Testament looks nothing like how we give today. In today's churches, giving constitutes filling out an auto-deposit form online so we can contribute our "biblical" ten percent to the central church fund to pay for all the salaries, programs, entertainment, and buildings.

We are *passive* givers.

What's interesting is that in the biblical context, tithing meant something entirely different. In the Old Testament, the tithe was essentially a three-part government income tax that totaled 23.3 percent. This tax was paid to fund the sponsorship of religious festivals in Jerusalem and to support the Levites, orphans, strangers, and widows (aka the poor). What's also interesting is that the tithe was paid almost entirely in the form of produce from the land, *not* in money.

In the New Testament era, Christians absolutely paid their taxes, but tithing as giving (as we understand it today) is nonexistent among the young Christian church. The first-century Christians were extraordinarily generous, but it was out of love, not obligation, that they gave.

For the first three centuries, the concept of tithing is completely absent from the Christian life. It isn't until the seventh and eighth centuries that we see the concept resurrected. Only in this case, Europe began to use the tithe, or the "tenth," as a way of defining land-lease payments to landowners. Initially, the majority of landowners were private citizens, but, over time, by way of government support, the church became the predominant landowner of the day, which meant the ten-percent lease payments began going instead to the Ecclesiastical leaders. By the end of the eighth century, this tithe had evolved into a *legal* requirement throughout most of Western Europe.

In both cases, tithing was much more akin to the income taxes we have in America today than benevolent giving for the advancement of God's kingdom.[6]

By contrast, in Acts 2:45 we see that the first Christians actively sought out need in their communities and neighborhoods and gave generously as they *saw* need. In other words, they gave because there was a *specific* need they were addressing, not because they were taught to "tithe" a specific amount of money to the community's central bank account. The only time the text refers to elders coordinating large sums of money is when the occasional wealthy person would sell their possessions and come to the apostles seeking input as to where the greatest need was.[7] Yet it seems to me that regardless of the circumstances, the members of the community were intimately involved in where they were giving and their generosity was always an answer to a specific need, not simply a call to fund a central bank account like we see today.

New Testament Christians were *active* givers.

And most importantly, they were giving to *people* who were in need. They weren't giving to support their own aspirations for *corporate* growth.

Comparing this with how tithing is discussed in churches today, the discrepancy seems quite glaring. Today, we're essentially taught as a community to blindly give to a central church pot, under the idea that we are required to tithe ten percent to the church and unwaveringly trust our leaders to steward those funds (which as I've discussed is not supported biblically). Under this practice, the leaders themselves not only have the autonomy to determine how the resources should be spent, but also, remarkably, the authority to determine their own honor (salaries).

There is a fundamental difference between people giving because they are told to give out of "faith" (so that leaders can *then* figure out where the entire community's donations are going and how much is going to themselves), and the image of giving the Bible paints: Christians recognizing a specific need an elder or member of the community might have, and giving to fulfill that need.

A direct answer to a direct need.

To give an example, the leaders of the large church my wife and I attend here in San Francisco recently shared their annual budget forecast for the coming year. They are budgeting a "need" of more than one million dollars to simply fund salaries and the renting of offices and an auditorium. Of the total budget, ten percent is going to "giving." (Which for them means church planting. Or, in other words, building more corporate franchises in other cities across the country.)

Corporate growth is not giving.

To me it seems a little ridiculous that we are spending over a million dollars this year just so a community of one thousand people can passively gather to hear someone preach and hear someone play guitar. According to this plan, we have to spend more than one million dollars on our own entertainment before we can even begin to address the *actual* needs that exist in our community.

What's even crazier is that, given the corporate model we've chosen, our church is actually run quite efficiently in comparison to our peers (I know of other churches whose annual budgets are well in excess of ten million dollars and spend close to a million dollars a year on lighting and sound production alone). But even as well as our church is run from a fiscal standpoint, I still don't think we come close to making responsible use of the resources we've been given.

Which makes me ask the question:

If we're running the church model we've chosen well and the church (read: corporation) is still consuming the overwhelming majority of the resources and time of the congregation, then doesn't that mean there is something fundamentally wrong with the model?

The whole model seems glaringly self-serving to me and very far from how the early Christians expressed and cultivated their faith. And I don't think I'm being subjective when I say this.

The numbers don't lie.

I understand that there are always going to be some costs with supporting, coordinating, and bringing together a community of any significant size, but I have a hard time believing that supporting ourselves should consume ninety percent of what we "give."

In fact, I think it should be the other way around. Ninety percent should be going directly to needs (either locally or globally) and ten percent to supporting the organizational aspects. We expect this from non-profits like World Vision, Compassion, and the Red Cross. Why do we not expect the same level of stewardship from our own churches — from ourselves?

This is why one of the areas I really think we need to

acknowledge and re-evaluate is how much pressure pastoral and staff salaries put on a congregation — as I'm not fully convinced this modern idea of a "professional" pastor exists in the Bible at all.[8] There were missionary church founders (like the apostle Paul) who were partially supported by the broader community who sent them out, but it was never explicitly expected or mandated.

Paul accepted gifts and support on occasion when he was planting a church in a new region, but he fully supported himself by and large through his tent-making business. He was intentionally self-sufficient because he didn't want to burden the people he was serving. In 1 Timothy, Paul talks at length about the topic of honoring elders. Though some believe the passage provides full justification for pastoral salaries, I believe it serves more as a call for the community of believers to "take care of," "support," and "respect" their elders. But, even then, I have a hard time believing that their need should be demanding as large of a percentage of the community's giving as it often does today. And I surely do not believe they should be given the autonomy to personally decide just how much "honor" they deserve.

I really think the entire issue comes down to the reality that the modern church places the bulk of its effort and money *internally* into teaching, preaching, music, and real estate — aka Sundays. Whereas Jesus, the disciples, and the rest of the early church spent the majority of their effort living out their faith *in homes and in the streets*. They lived lives that were discipleship focused, as opposed to classroom focused. Knowledge came through their experiences in action, not academic knowledge pushing them into action, as we try to do today.

We've flipped Jesus' example upside down in almost every way.

Jesus didn't even have a place to lay His head, let alone a corporate office full of staff managing His ministry, or a huge auditorium to share His message. In fact, He came to abolish temple building entirely. Paul was able to plant the global church almost entirely on a self-supported basis. If they were able to do more with less, and we truly aim to be disciples of Christ, we should to.

PAYCHECKS IN THE NAME OF JESUS

What I find even more interesting is that if you speak to pastors about these convictions (as I have several times), most, if not all, will say they agree with you. They'll even preach minimalism from the stage. Yet we continue to build and build and build. Why the hypocrisy?

For me the short answer is simple: survival.

Pastors can agree with me all they want (and maybe even deep down they really do), but there's no escaping the fact that they, their families, their reputation, their livelihood, all hinge on the success of the corporation (church). Their paychecks, programs, facilities, and ability to attract top-notch "talent" only exist if tithing attendees exist.

The business needs income.

It's an incredibly complex conflict of interest, but also a convenient solution for the masses of attendees (me included) who would rather write a check than truly invest our time, efforts, or emotions into a truly biblical expression of church.

For pastors it's a very precarious position to be in. One that I don't envy in the slightest because I personally know how hard (impossible?) it is to walk that tight rope. When I left Las Vegas, and was still jobless, I launched a non-profit organization called SWL (Speak With Love), where we used apparel sales and live concerts to raise resources and awareness for starving children and child sex slaves.

We kept the company afloat by keeping a portion of the profit from the clothing sales (the majority of the profit, I confess). We then gave the remaining percentage to the charities we worked with. For example, we would sell a shirt that cost us $7 for $20 and donate $3 of our $13 profit to charity. Under this revenue split, only 15% of the revenue we generated (or 23% of the profits) were going towards the causes we were "supporting" — which didn't feel like enough.

Over time, I found it increasingly difficult to manage my own need to make money with my heart's polar desire to give more and more of the proceeds away, because unfortunately, when you're in personal survival mode, self-preservation is always going to kick in. And that's exactly what happened with me. Not able to afford to give more of it away, and unable to fully resolve the angst I was feeling about how little we were actually giving away, I forced myself to shut the company down. I shut it down because

I wasn't serving either beneficiary (myself or the charity) well.

I could never escape the reality that the true reason we were giving at all was for our own gain. The giving was nothing more than a clever marketing angle. It was an entirely self-serving enterprise cloaked in a touching message. And even though we arguably did some good, I still feel like we perverted the purity of the causes we supported by disproportionately benefiting ourselves on each sale.

I came to the conclusion that the only way the organization could be run ethically was if I could do it without seeking any material gain from it. It would have to be purely benevolent. I don't think a "feed Travis" project and a "feed the kids" project can be one in the same.

The conflict between self-preservation and honest benevolence is too much to escape. But it's the exact conflict that exists in every corporate church in America today.

In today's corporate church system, if we want to be one-hundred percent sold out on Jesus and give one-hundred percent of our time to Him — aka "give our lives to ministry," the only way is to become a financial burden on the entire community of believers we desire to serve.

Under our current definition of church, our "generosity" and "sacrifice," interestingly, translate into real-world *income* for us, and real-world *debt* for everyone else.

In America, serving has become a career.

As conflicting as this seems, we justify this as bodies of believers by saying things like, "There's so many things that need to be done; we *need* someone to be full-time." But the question we really need to ask ourselves is this: Are all those things we're doing truly about *being* the church, or about building a corporation we're *calling* a church?

I don't think it was Jesus' intention for us to become burdens on those we are called to serve. I can't help but believe Paul set the example of being a tentmaker for a reason.

If you think about it, the formula is quite simple:

If we truly want to serve more people, then we need to learn how to make more tents.

If I can have a full-time job, invest fully in a mid-week small group, participate on Sundays, and donate my time to the needs of the church throughout the week then surely others (like teachers and elders) can too. But that's only if we are willing to throw away the empire-building mentality of church of which we're all a part. Corporations will always provide us with things to do and manage. But Christ doesn't call us to build or manage. He calls us to live out our identity in Christ and spread His love to the ends of the earth.[9]

That's it.

Nothing else.

Period.

We are so indoctrinated with the idea that there should be "professional" ministers that we forget to actually look to the Bible where Paul himself managed to plant the global church and write the vast majority of the New Testament, all while keeping a job to provide for himself in almost every case. He provided for himself while still giving his entire mind, body, and spirit to his Christ-given mission to spread the church throughout the known world.

Paul was not a burden, despite having quite a bit more responsibility on his shoulders than our modern-day pastors.

If he was able to find a way, so can we.

And the good news is, some people already are.

ALTERNATIVE CHURCH (WE ARE THE CHURCH)

The table that follows is adapted from the book *Revolution* by George Barna.[10] This is the table that broke the whole world open for me. We often hear in the news and media that Christianity is dying in America today. If you haven't seen the research and only read the headlines, it might very well seem this way, but this graphic tells us something entirely different.

The Christian church (and by "church," I mean community)

HOW AMERICANS EXPERIENCE AND EXPRESS THEIR FAITH
Primary means of spiritual experience and expression

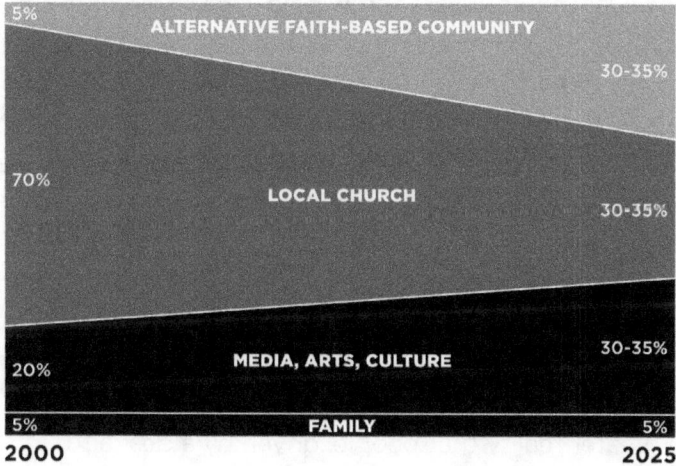

5%	ALTERNATIVE FAITH-BASED COMMUNITY
	30-35%
70%	LOCAL CHURCH
	30-35%
	30-35%
20%	MEDIA, ARTS, CULTURE
5%	FAMILY
2000	5%
	2025

in America isn't dying, it's *changing*.

Changing might even be too soft of a word here. Based on the data, the church in America is experiencing an all-out disruption. A complete redefinition of the status quo on par with what the internet, and Amazon in particular, have done to brick and mortar retail, or what iTunes and Spotify have done to the music industry. The institutional church as we know it today is deteriorating at an astounding rate. According to the data, by 2025 the percentage of Christians whose primary means of spiritual experience and expression is through a local church (read: corporate church) is going to fall from 70% to 30%, with the people in flux transitioning almost entirely to alternative faith-based communities (think organic or home-based churches, cell groups, affinity groups of believers, etc.)

But why?

Not because people are throwing away Christianity, but because they are throwing away the *model* of Christianity that has been constructed over the past several hundred years. A definition of Christianity where the word "church" no longer refers to the global community of believers that God has "set apart" and Jesus came to save (*ekklesia*), but has evolved to represent corporate growth alongside the name of Jesus (and I mean corporate in the business sense of the word).

Instead of settling for this spin on Acts, this table reveals the greater reality that people, driven by a desire to express their faith in ways that more closely and intimately resemble the true heart of Acts, are abandoning the modern-day paradigms of the local Christian church. They are pursuing lives that resonate more deeply with the true heart and vision Jesus and His disciples' held when they wrote the word *ekklesia* some two thousand years ago: *a global community of believers coming together and intimately sharing life with one another, growing deeper in understanding of God's love for them, and closer in relationship with our Lord and Savior, Jesus Christ.*

Jesus' entire ministry centered around one message: *we are the church.* The heart of God, of Jesus, lives *in* us. We are the temple. *There is nothing to build.*

No temples.

No idols.

We are simply called to live in community with one another and share the "Good News" (the Gospel) with the rest of the world who is not yet "set apart" by and for God.

Does the local church today help build communities of believers? Yes. Does the local church today help share the Gospel with the world? Yes. Can brilliant musicians lead us into deep worship of our Lord? Yes. Can brilliant pastors stir our hearts and bring the Word of God to life? Absolutely. Is the model of the local church, as we experience it today, the *only* way for Christians to build community, worship God, and share the love of God with the world? No.

Let me repeat. No.

Absolutely, emphatically, no.

Could the people who make up our nation of local churches today be more effective in sharing life together and reaching the lost world if they were less focused on *building* a "church," and more focused on actually *being* the church in our neighborhoods and cities?

I would venture to say yes.

The latter is how millions of American Christians are choosing to live out their faith, in lieu of the pageantry. To be clear, droves of people aren't walking away from local churches because they are walking away from God, they are walking away from traditional congregations because they are seeking *more* of God. They are seeking true, New Testament community. Community on mission. Community without all the worldly construction.

And they are finding it.[11]

Do you know what the early believers called themselves? They simply identified themselves as, "The Church at (Insert City)."

The Church at Jerusalem.
The Church at Ephesus.
The Church at Corinth.

Notice it's not "a" church, but "the" church. As in *one* church. The one church Jesus commissioned as He ascended into Heaven. No clever names. No flashy logos. No catchy tag lines. No rock bands. Not even an address.

Just like Jesus.[12]

Why?

Because their sole purpose was to follow Him. They were set on fire by the truth, not clever marketing. They were set free, not imprisoned by a commission to build. They understood there was nothing to build, because they understood the church was *in* them.

What if all the church names, congregations, and denominations that hold us captive today were all stripped away and replaced with the New Testament nomenclature?

Imagine how much *freedom* that would create.

In the New Testament diaspora, members of the church, Jesus' church (read: community of believers whom He'd "set apart"), gathered together across multiple homes, venues, locations, cities, nations, and in multiple ways, yet all with *one* identity. In the midst of the swelling crowds, they didn't begin pooling their money and efforts to build temples so they could gather together in better fashion or function, or divide themselves into clashing teams. They simply gathered together, in increasing numbers of mostly small, home-based gatherings, to grow closer in communion with each other and God. Then they, as *individual* members of Christ's body, gave their resources to bless those people in their cities and neighborhoods who were in need.

Their spiritual lives were fluid, which stands in stark contrast to the highly structured, rigid, and fragmented paradigms and dogmas that defines us today.

New Testament believers didn't derive their identity from the catchy name and logo that hung above the hall where they gathered, or the quality of the band they'd assembled, or the number of people who attended. Their identities were rooted in the redeeming love of Jesus. That's it. They focused their entire lives on further connecting with this love and sharing Jesus with the world. And it was that focus that set the world ablaze.

It's hard for a community to live outwardly, when the largest draw of a community's time, effort, and resources is inward — consumed by the maintenance of the corporate edifice, officers, and weekly "entertainment."

I want to be clear. Preaching and teaching of the Word is wonderful. It's imperative. So are worship music and the arts. So is gathering together to do both of these things. Yet I think spending the majority of the week and the vast majority of our resources (more than ninety percent in most cases) paying for preachers, musicians, artists, and venues is missing the point.

Paying for people to use their spiritual gifts should not consume the vast majority of our resources.

For example, one of my spiritual gifts is design. I used to give several hours a week in efforts to the church plant we were a part of. In that same several hours, the pastor who is (hopefully) spiritually gifted in teaching can develop a sermon for the week. Yet we "buy" the pastor's time (and the venue for him to preach in) through our tithes, while we as the congregation are expected to give of ours. Why is there a double standard?

If God is calling you to preach, preach.

We don't need pulpits, buildings, or even live, in-person crowds to facilitate preaching of the Gospel.[13] Podcasts are free. Blogs are free. Building community and assembling the church is free because our living rooms and public spaces are free (or at least already paid for). If it's *really* about teaching, we don't need any of the material things we often use as justification for needing a venue. If we are part of a community of three hundred people we most likely have more than two hundred homes that can be used as venues. Yet, for some reason, in the modern-day church, a home doesn't qualify as a venue anymore.

Jesus cares most about discipleship, and discipleship

happens in small, intimate community — realistically in groups of no more than twelve people (I like to think Jesus chose twelve disciples for a reason). And real life happens one on one. So, if this is true, then why are we spending the vast majority of our collective time, effort, and resources on venues, performers, and concerts with a spiritual monologue in the middle, when the core of the Christian experience exists outside of all that?

I've really been pressing into this question lately, and I've come to the conclusion that it's because the modern-day church model, driven by the pursuit of relevancy, has adapted itself to a consumerist and entertainment-driven collection of believers who would rather push the easy button and passively attend a weekly show, write a check, and go about the rest of their week.

Consuming believers like me.

People like me are the problem. Even though we can sense the growing apathy in our hearts, our rhetoric sounds much, much different — because, for better or worse, us Christians have become experts at putting on a good show. But it's hard to believe in our empty statements because our actions (and dollars) speak for themselves.

Follow our money, follow our time, and it's easy to see where our priorities are. The modern-day church has effectively taken what it means to be the church out of the hearts of the people and wrapped it around the shoulders of paid professionals. So much so that we've come to believe that we are unqualified to meet amongst fellow believers without the watchful guidance of one of these "professionals" and under the banner of the accompanying organization. We as God's people have essentially surrendered our God-given priesthood.

This is sad.

We have become so removed from our biblical identity as believers, as saints, that we are actually afraid to meet on our own — to be *Christian* on our own. And if we are actually brave enough to step out, we are relentlessly discouraged and warned by the "professionals" we've appointed that we lack the expertise to navigate those waters on our own.

For example, I've shared multiple times with pastors that I have a desire to organize a small gathering of fellow believers for the simple purpose of creating community on a more intimate scale, only to be warned, cautioned, coached, that, "It's dangerous to meet without proper supervision." I find it really frustrating when all I want to do is seek God in the company of my peers and instead of receiving encouragement, I am instructed to seek out a chaperon like a sixth-grader who wants to go to the movies.

Jesus gave His life by being brutally nailed to a cross, where He bled, suffocated, and died, so that we might be restored and have the freedom to seek a direct and intimate relationship with Him. Yet today we spend our weekends standing in aisles of modern-day temples, holding out field trip permission slips for our pastors to sign.

Feels a lot like arrested spiritual development to me.

I want to be clear. I wholeheartedly believe it is crucial to have solid believers in your life with whom you can hold each other accountable. But I don't think you need someone with a degree in theology or a job title to officiate and facilitate your spiritual life. God calls us to seek communion with Him and with fellow believers. That's it. No rules. No mediators.

We mustn't forget that it is *God* who raises up elders, not men.

Donald Miller wrote a wonderful parable recently that does a great job of highlighting just how much the local church has disenfranchised and discouraged the power we have as individual believers. I didn't want to include it in its entirety here, but take ten minutes and read it now. (The link is in the end notes)[14]

Let us not forget, or let anyone convince us otherwise, that *we are the church.*

God is available and present every time we call upon him. Period. God operates under a very simple promise, "If you seek, you will find."[15] And our mission is simple:

We are called to seek the Lord with all our hearts, live in communion with other believers, and carry the message of His love to the ends of the earth.[16]

Our hearts should be free to seek Him and follow Him, in whatever direction He calls us to, and in any form He sees fit. Free from the burdensome and self-edifying belief that our calling to be an active participant in Christ's church means building modern-day temples and corporations.

Freedom of spirit and heart is the only life God wants for us. Our current paradigm is eroding at the seams because people are desperately seeking to find Jesus for real — because the largely diluted version of Christianity many of our churches are offering isn't enough. Make no mistake, God absolutely loves His church. He loves the *people* who are "set apart" in His name. But I'm not as convinced that He's in love with the model we've built around our faith.

There are no churches to build.

I think it deserves to be said a second time.

There are no churches to build.

The only church on this planet is the one that exists in our collective hearts — the one Jesus lived, died, and rose again to create. We are His church because He lives *within* us and impacts the world *through* us. Our call isn't to build but to carry the message of His love to the world through the *entirety* of our lives.

I now realize why church has felt like nothing more than a tremendous weight on my soul for much of my life: because it's not church at all. A life created apart from God is heavy because it rests entirely on our shoulders. A life created and lead by God is exhilaratingly light.[17]

I've let the world put church *on* me. But even more so, *I've* put church on myself.

It's time to be free.

No more guilt.
No more chains.
No more building.

It's time to embrace the freedom we all have to seek God's love and experience the excitement of sharing His freeing love with the world.

Now, that feels right.

WHAT NOW?

What I've found to be the most interesting result of my release of the paradigm of church that I've been holding onto so tightly is the vast surplus of time, energy, emotional, and financial resources I now have to give to the callings God has placed on my heart. No longer are my weeks full of obligations, the never ending burden of building and maintaining all that we've already built, the dull pain deep inside my soul, the angst of the friction signaling there's something more in store for my life — for all our lives.

Yet it's in this space, the vacancy that walking away from empire building has created, that I, for the first time in my life, truly feel like God has an opportunity to do something *through me*. I feel as though I'm looking at the world for the first time, with brand new eyes. I feel as though He's opening my heart to the life He's intended for me all along.

But in the space there are also many questions:

What does it look like to be a member of His church, *the* church?
What does it mean to give when there's no longer a religious corporation to give to?
What does organic community look like?

What do I do now?

CHURCH UNPLUGGED (A MANIFESTO)

It's an interesting question. And in my newfound sense of freedom I've been really seeking to understand at a deeper level what it truly means to live as a disciple of Christ.

In the end, I've come to believe that the Christian life really comes down to three central purposes:

1. Love the Lord your God with all your heart[18]
2. Love your Neighbor as yourself[19]
3. Make disciples[20]

The simplicity almost seems ridiculous, doesn't it? Especially when you compare it to the overwhelmingly complex world of corporate churches and never-ending theological debates with which we are so familiar.

I want to also note that I wrote them in a specific order, because I believe each comes with increasing intimacy with

God and spiritual wisdom. It takes the love of God in your heart to be able to pour that out onto others, and even more intimacy of relationship with God, and vastly greater commitment, to lead others in their walk with God.

Just think, it took Jesus, the Creator of the Universe, three years of daily mentorship to prepare His twelve disciples. If it took the Son of God three years of daily investment, imagine the level of commitment and depth of relationships we must have with Jesus and each other to even begin to do the same.

I've spent a lot of time talking with various believers close to me about what a Christian life free of church building might actually look like. With the goal of not being overly prescriptive, here's my vision, my manifesto, for what an "unplugged" spiritual life might look like:

■ ■ ■

A MANIFESTO

SIMPLICITY:

Our mission is to return to a simpler way of living out our faith. A life grounded in the stories of Acts, in intimate community — in focus.

SUNDAYS:

We need to completely re-imagine what it means to gather together on Sundays — and be honest with ourselves about the exorbitant amount of resources being consumed by the paid staff and buildings required to produce it in it's current form. We need to let go of the pageantry and seek ways to gather without making it such a burden on the community. Our goal should be to use ten percent of our efforts and resources towards facilitating corporate community and ninety percent towards interpersonal relationships and addressing the needs of people and our communities.

COMMUNITY:

We are a network of small (no more than twelve people) "cell" groups who meet together weekly, both as a group and one on one throughout the week. A "Fight Club" of believers, we gather in our homes, share meals together, pray, study the Word, invest into each others lives and God-given pursuits, carry one another in the midst of struggles, and celebrate one another's victories. We are prayer warriors, confidants, and friends.

We are family.

Being active in our faith is the foundation of our community. Our goal is not to become a stagnant intellectual center.

In the end everything boils down to one goal: *create a community that raises up disciples who make disciples*.

(In addition to the core "cell" groups, I am also really interested in creating a weekly gathering of like-minded Christian creatives who simply gather together to share a meal, collaborate, and work on our individual projects. I think of it as a creative hack night. And my hope is to connect believers around affinities, passions, and interests with the common mission of making Jesus famous through the entirety of our lives.)

WORSHIP & PREACHING:

If enough "cell" groups exist in a similar area or city, I think it would be wonderful to come together as neighborhoods on a weekly basis and as a collective community (including all communities and churches of any affiliation in our city) on a semi-regular basis (say about once a month). It would be a great time to share struggles, successes, and victories, as well as take part in corporate worship and preaching. It would be a time of celebration and unification. A time to remind ourselves we are all a part of the greater story of redemption God is ever telling.

Depending on the size of the broader community, to facilitate a semi-regular gathering we will leverage either a donated location or rent a space for that night *only*, where people can give to cover the specific costs — nothing more. All costs and financial details will be completely public and no gifts in excess of what is needed will be accepted.

All general teaching that happens outside of the collective gathering, by elders and those whose spiritual gift it is to preach, will be delivered digitally via podcasts and live streams. All this media, as well as a directory of "cell" groups, will be centralized online so anyone can get connected with fellow believers in their city and access all the media that's being created.

The goal is to leverage the affordability, scalability, and portability the Internet provides to eliminate all the overhead traditional models require.

GIVING:

Aside from specifically identified facilities needs (i.e. the space for the semi-regular gathering), there will be no central, corporate-related overhead or tithing to speak of. Giving will be an individual effort or self-organized by "cell" groups. We do not believe the idea of a ten percent tithe is biblical and instead believe we should be actively seeking to generously address needs in our communities *directly,* as they arise.

As a community, we find needs first, *then* seek to meet that need. There will be no corporate accumulation of wealth or material things.

STAFF:

There will be zero professional or paid staff required because there is no corporation to run. Simply "cell" group hosts, leaders, and elders who feel called to help disciple others. Living out our faith is not a profession, but a calling we all share as believers.

ACTS 1:8:

As part of our calling to make disciples and spread the message of Jesus, we will seek to help anyone who is interested in starting a "cell" group in their area.

Our desire is to spread the Gospel through one-on-one relationships. We are not a mass-marketing machine. We believe the Gospel will spread on its own, as a result of focus and God's will.

. . .

Imagine if we lived this way. Imagine if I, and the one thousand other people I attend church with, lived this way. Imagine what kind of impact the millions of dollars we spend on ourselves every year could do in this city. Imagine what kind of impact the hundreds of billions of dollars we give to *ourselves* every year on a national and global scale could have if we *actually* gave it away.

The answer is simple: a lot.

Think of the effect we could have on the hearts of people if we gave our lives recklessly for the benefits of others.

If we have the courage to do it, the world might even stop labeling us with words like "hypocritical" and "judgmental," and start identifying us with one the label we all long to embody:

Christians.

CREATION (AND FREEDOM) REQUIRES DEATH

Now I realize much of what I've said is a huge departure from "normal." But as my own initial shock to the disruption has subsided, I've come to realize that the dramatic shifts that are happening are *critical* to the vibrancy of the global church.

Despite our resistance to it, *change is necessary*.

Our universe breathes through the inhale and exhale of seasons. Did you know the human body completely recreates and replaces every single one of its roughly ten trillion cells every seven years? Some organs in your body are replaced every few weeks. Seriously. Every single cell in your body right now is less than seven years old. And to make way for those ten trillion new cells, the original cells were all replaced. Every. Single. One. Gone.

In order to make room for the new, the old must pass away.

Before spring can come, there must first be winter. But despite its necessity, enduring the losses of winter is beyond difficult. The separation from the present incarnation of beauty our hearts so dearly cling to is painful. It stretches our souls to the breaking point, as our minds crisscross the possibility that the promises of the coming spring might all be empty.

But spring never disappoints, because we are all swept up in the swell of an epic story our Creator is telling and ever-moving forward. A story of redemption.

A story He has promised to finish.

Whether we understand the context of the ever-fleeting time we've been given in this life or not, the story is ever advancing, building into a crescendo, as spring continues to live up to its promise. The Good News is the promise that the story doesn't end in the barren, bitter cold of winter's grasp, but in the glory of summer's freedom and warmth.

Experiencing the temporality of our world is not easy, especially in the areas we're able to control most. We are forced to accept the seasonal weather of our planet, but the seasonality of our own creation is not as easy to embrace. We impart a small piece of ourselves into everything we create, everything we bring into being. So it is with great difficulty that we must, as creators, give of ourselves knowing that, in time, we must, too, die to ourselves in order to make room for the inevitable revival of our own creation.

But more than our hearts cleave to what we create, our pride, our egos, our paradigms, tightly weave themselves around it, too. For some of us, this enmeshment, this tangled mess of attachment, proves too much to sort out. We are trapped in the antiquity of our own creations. Frozen by a winter we refuse to let pass. We see the casualties of this resistance to the advancement of God's story every day. Governments, corporations, and churches are all being overthrown constantly by spring's unrelenting creativity and growth.

As a creator, it's important to understand the realities that surround what it means to create. The privilege of creating the new also brings with it the responsibility of causing the downfall of the old. And we must create with the humility and understanding that our creation, too, stands to ultimately experience the same fate.

Ashes to ashes. Dust to dust.[21]

So, if all of this is true, if the entire universe operates under the same ebb and flow of seasons, why do we find it so difficult to accept the same death and rebirth of our communities of faith (aka churches)?

Why do we resist change from within so intensely?
Why do we hate to see instances of the church close their doors?
Why do we fight so desperately to keep them alive?

We fight because death hurts. Especially when it's something we've worked so hard to create. Something we've poured ourselves out countless times for. It hurts because part of who we are lives in what we've created.

Despite our love of them, the local churches in our communities are not immune to seasons. Our communities of faith must evolve, adapt, grow — and even die, too. This is why we must hold our communities loosely. We must give God the freedom to break, rebuild, mold, and manifest His will for our lives through the inspiration and expression of our hearts. Our communities should always be in process, because *we* should always be in process.

With this in mind, I can't help but believe our denial of change is creating atrophy in the Christian faith today — I know it has in my own life. I've spent my entire life holding onto antiquated and broken ideas of what "church" is supposed to be and I am exposing my heart in these pages because I believe there are way too many people trapped by the standing relics we still defend as real community. All the energy we could be spending on reviving and creating a renewed community of faith is being wasted holding up a fractured system. And because we can't find it in ourselves to let go, we remain stuck, stagnate, doing everything we can to embalm the paradigms that have held up our lives for too long.

Why do so many of us allow ourselves to believe that spending one hour on Sunday in a room with a thousand strangers is what it means to follow Jesus?

No matter what we tell ourselves, it's not.

I don't know about you, but a thousand people scattered across a city, radically living out what it means to be a disciple of Jesus, and meeting intimately to discuss the nuances of their lives and struggles feels a lot more like real community to me.

I think if we lived this way, the outside world may start using nicer words to describe us Christians; words that more accurately express the gloriously good intentions and desires we all have to serve Jesus.

I think this version of church is possible.

In fact, as I've shared, it's already emerging.[22]

It's igniting from the friction that exists between the modern-day church, the secular world, and a generation of believers who are longing for something more than the lives we are living.

Tomorrow's church exists in those pangs, in the burning creativity and desires God has placed on our hearts, the desires He has woven into our souls.

Spring is coming.

And it's coming by way of our divinely imparted creativity.

SET FREE

As I look back now on my life and all that God has done to intercede on my behalf, the more I'm beginning to really understand God's heart, His mission:

He's trying to set us free.

It's as if we're lost in the middle of a briar patch and He's lashing His way through, fighting for our lives, our souls. Our desperation is so great, the brokenness so severe, we are not even capable of fighting for ourselves. And so He comes to our rescue. Again. And again. And again.

And He will keep coming for us and unbinding the chains we shackle around our lives and souls. God's pursuit of us and love for us are relentless because the world, Satan, and our rebellion, are relentless.

Even more profoundly, God frees us because He desires for us to collaborate with Him. He desires for us to take part in the advancement of His story and the rescuing of lost souls

— a call only a free heart can answer. Our freedom isn't the end goal, it is barely the beginning.

God frees us for a simple yet unfathomable purpose: *so that He can work through us to set others free.* God is forever inviting us, calling us, commanding us, to fight for the souls of our brothers and sisters. Being a member of God's *ekklesia* is not a spectator sport. We have a central role to play in His story.[23]

We are called to be vessels.

And I believe at the core of who we are, all that God has designed us to be, being in the midst of this divine mission is the only place where we will ever truly experience life, purpose, and fulfillment.

God says, "Come to me and I will give you life."[24] And life exists in our active participation in the redemption of God's creation and His church. God draws us into this story by moving through our lives, our creativity, and our communities. I believe God has blessed each and every one of us with specific skills and talents because He has a divine intention to use them for the redemption of all mankind.

I believe God is constantly playing a symphony with our passions, masterfully crafting a melody for the salvation of lost souls and His glory, *through* His church — through us.

But only if we can find the courage within ourselves to let Him.

A REVOLUTION

In the undertow of all these swirling convictions, resting at the base of my soul, is the somber reality that, despite my heart's desire for transformation, my entire life has been marked more by attendance than an active life reflective of Jesus. It's quite sad actually. Troubling. Pathetic. Especially in contrast to the rebelliously free and convicting life Jesus gave His life for and the radical, subversive mission He's ever inviting us into.

Lost in the seemingly endless cycle of lectures that the Christian life has largely become (the academic life I helped create), I feel so stagnant, so listless.[25]

Bogged down in the bureaucracy, dogma, and predominantly inward-facing edification of my own salvation, I've become trapped in my own head. I've traded in walking the streets and connecting intimately in living rooms, for sitting in classrooms and auditoriums shoulder to shoulder with complete strangers, content to leave the real work to the professionals.

It's really embarrassing to admit just how *inactive* of a faith I live. I think Jesus would be quite disappointed with the lack of fruit my life has produced up to this point. Maybe filling these pages are my way of trying to wake myself up.

I love the title of Rob Bell's book *Jesus Wants to Save Christians Too* because it's a stark reminder that self-attributed Christianity doesn't exempt me, or any of us, from needing redemption.

Having been blessed to live in a nation of such incredible wealth, it's so hard to let go of the easy and comfortable Christian life we've created for ourselves. And because the thought of letting go is so utterly terrifying, we hold on to everything we've built for dear life, scared that letting go will cause the entirety of our faith to come crashing to the ground. The irony is, though, it's only in letting go of the materialism, construction, and capitalism that largely defines our expressions of faith that we can ever truly experience Jesus and the life He promises us.

We've become prisoners to our own comfort.

If you think about it, Satan is truly brilliant. Instead of simply keeping people away from the church, he's tricked all of us into focusing our time, money, and effort upon our own selves, our buildings, our events, our programs — in the *name* of church. We love our polished bands and video production and fancy lighting, yet outside the world continues to fall further into disarray. And without a clue in the world, we fall asleep at night thinking we're living a life that echoes the life of our Savior.

The comfort is so numbing it's making me desperate for something, anything, that's raw and unvarnished. I don't want to be comfortable anymore. I want to experience the full gradient of pain and joy, Heaven and Hell, that is found in the life Jesus is beckoning all of us into.

As convicted as I am, though, I'm finding it so incredibly difficult to walk away from the comfort. It takes unimaginable courage to truly give your life to Jesus. It's like my soul is playing tug of war with my humanity. But in the midst of the tension, it's so encouraging to know there are people out there who have found the courage to let go.

That's why George Barna's chart is so amazing to me. It proves there are millions of people who are letting go of the amenity-laden ways of old, and embracing the dynamic life Jesus promises us. And with their decisions, they are ushering in the sunrise of new (or should I say "old"?) ways to carry the light of the Gospel into the world.

There is hope.

And it's exciting. Because the moment we realize that God is moving mountains before our eyes, the conversation immediately becomes less about who we are today as a global church and more about the good news of who we are *becoming.*

And maybe that's the key. This entire conversation is not really about the present fracturing of the status quo, but the need to celebrate the budding movement of souls desperately seeking to return to the liberating life God intends for us. A revolution is emerging within God's *ekklesia,* right before our very eyes.

Jesus is making "all things new."[26]

FILTERING ABANDONMENT

In the wake of all I've just shared, in the midst of my excitement for the ways God is moving, I must admit that my heart is aching. It's struggling to absorb the immense reality that millions of people are choosing to leave existing communities of believers in hopes of finding or creating new ones.

I can tell you from experience, separation from the greater body of believers can be a lonely and dangerous place — albeit necessary at times. Though stepping away can be the right decision, thinking of the waves of abandonment makes me long for the restoration of the communities God has already assembled.

God has already gathered His *ekklesia* together in massive fashion and I think it would be a great tragedy for that to be fractured beyond recognition. I do concede, though, that there are times where, in order to restore them, God must break communities just as He does souls — but I can't help but hold tightly to the hope that restoration *within* our existing bodies of believers is possible, too.

As anyone who's remodeled a house can attest, changing the existing is always considerably more messy than building something new. But even then, we can't let the messiness distort the reality that creation and restoration are *equally* daunting pursuits, because people are *always* messy.

It's easy to fall into the trap of wanting to pick "teams," but I don't believe this is, or should ever be, an either-or dilemma.

I think the answer is "both."

We must learn to celebrate the formation of new communities of faith and the restoration of the existing in the same breath. There is incredible possibility and beauty in both directions. We must open our hearts to the joy of witnessing the expansion and evolution of God's Kingdom before our eyes across the *full* gradient of His work.

As I've mentioned throughout this book, we must edit our lives. We need to edit our churches too. As I've also mentioned, being an editor is incredibly hard — especially when peoples' hearts, beliefs, and emotions are involved. This is why "re-modeling" is such difficult work.

But we cannot confuse "difficult" with "impossible" or "fruitless."

I've spent weeks trying to find peace with my convictions as they relate to the status quo that is the modern-day church. A group of us gathered together several times over those same weeks to explore what *ekklesia* truly means (much of which was inspired by what I've talked about in this book) with the hope of better connecting and reconciling our convictions with the larger body of believers in our city and avoiding the collateral tendency to abandon the community of people as a result of our desire to abandon some of the paradigms that confine it. After several weeks of in-depth discussion, we came to a critical conclusion:

We must separate the model, the paradigms, from the people.

And in the space created by that realization, a seven-principle vision of what a community in pursuit of true *ekklesia* might look like emerged:

1. One-anothering (minister to one another and tend one another's needs, make disciples)

2. Foster the expression of the Gospel through our lives and divinely-given talents (both individually and collectively, see Luke 19:12-27 and Acts 1:8)

3. Commitment to accountability and reconciliation (as described in Matthew 18)

4. Minimalism with purpose (both individually and collectively)

5. Live as a family throughout the week (both in smaller groups and collectively - don't just do church together, do life together)

6. Missional (Radical generosity with our time and resources)

7. Prayerful (deep devotion to prayer and the seeking of God's leadership — both individually and collectively)

As simple as it reads, I can't deny the resolution my heart feels when I read over the list. For me, it seems to capture what it means to be a Christian — what the stories in Acts say about the values our lives should reflect. And it's through this mosaic of perspectives, this lens, that I feel God has provided a filter to help my heart, and hopefully, our hearts, make sense of where we are today and the direction, the purpose, our hearts should be fixated on as followers and vessels of Jesus.

It's become my compass.

Applying this filter to my own life has been a truly humbling experience. The glaring discrepancy between my own life and what it means to live out *ekklesia* is hard to reconcile. It makes me realize just how much I need God's strength and leadership in my life.

I desperately want to be called a Christian because others identify my actions with that of Christ, not because I've attributed the designation to myself. I hold this same desire for us collectively, too. And I believe if we truly fix our hearts on the vigilant pursuit of *ekklesia* in our lives and communities, the world will take note as God's undeniable brilliance pours itself out through His church — through us.

So it's with an expectant, humble, and hopeful heart, that I pray we as a global church will have the courage to hold a filter up to our own lives, hearts, and communities — and, more urgently, the conviction to press deeper into the pursuit of the lives God is calling us to.

It's the only way the world will ever come to know what *ekklesia* truly means.

FIVE
CHOOSE LIFE

———

"And the time came when the risk to remain tight in a bud was more painful than the risk it took to blossom."

—Anaïs Nin

———

CHOOSE LIFE

For a while now, I've had a difficult time finding an ending for this story. These pages have remained blank for weeks, as I've struggled to keep pace with the fleeting sense of closure I've been chasing.

After much introspection, I've come to think that maybe it doesn't need to end. Maybe there isn't supposed to be a specific answer because God's answer for our purpose in life is unique for each one of us.

It's also been difficult to find resolution in all of this because I can't help but feel like this book is really only the beginning. This book is the first thing I've ever created that I truly care about to the depths of my being. Even though it terrifies me to think about it, I've done my best to pour my soul into these pages — and I hope, despite my demons, the result is good, positive, and uplifting. If you feel I didn't succeed, I'm truly sorry.

In all of this there is one thing I do know, though. Having now experienced what it feels like to create from a place of such intimacy with myself, with God, with such a sense of vulnerability, I'll never be the same — life will never be the same.

Jason Fried, the founder of 37signals, has a great quote on his Twitter profile: "It's simple until you make it complicated." We humans are brilliant at making things complicated.

In the face of our natural tendency to muddle, we need

to always hold on to the truth that the number one thing Jesus desires for each and every one of us is simple: *life*. And He wants us to live life empowered by the freedom and creativity His vast love and grace gives us.

I can't even begin to tell you how many times in my life I've allowed my mind's endless stream of "what-ifs" to paralyze me — to prevent me from actually taking action and moving forward. As much as our minds love to deliberate hypotheticals, the reality is that we don't have the slightest idea what tomorrow is going to bring, or how the world will respond (or not) to our next creative pursuit.

There is only one thing certain in this life:

Inaction = Failure

Every. Single. Time.

God doesn't call us to be idle. God doesn't call us to play it safe. He calls us to move, to create, to succeed, to fail — in faith. It's the only hope we have of ever experiencing the life God desires for us. And as Jesus stresses in Luke 19, cowering to our fear and living a cautious life is not an option if we long to truly serve God:

THE PARABLE OF THE TEN MINAS

11 While they were listening to this, he went on to tell them a parable, because he was near Jerusalem and the people thought that the kingdom of God was going to appear at once. 12 He said: "A man of noble birth went to a distant country to have himself appointed king and then to return.

13 So he called ten of his servants and gave them ten minas. 'Put this money to work,' he said, 'until I come back.' 14 "But his subjects hated him and sent a delegation after him to say, 'We don't want this man to be our king.' 15 "He was made king, however, and returned home. Then he sent for the servants to whom he had given the money, in order to find out what they had gained with it. 16 "The first one came and said, 'Sir, your mina has earned ten more.' 17 "'Well done, my good servant!' his master replied. 'Because you have been trustworthy in a very small matter, take charge of ten cities.' 18 "The second came and said, 'Sir, your mina has earned five more.' 19 "His master answered, 'You take charge of five cities.' 20 "Then another servant came and said, 'Sir, here is your mina; I have kept it laid away in a piece of cloth. 21 I was afraid of you, because you are a hard man. You take out what you did not put in and reap what you did not sow.' 22 "His master replied, 'I will judge you by your own words, you wicked servant! You knew, did you, that I am a hard man, taking out what I did not put in, and reaping what I did not sow? 23 Why then didn't you put my money on deposit, so that when I came back, I could have collected it with interest?' 24 "Then he said to those standing by, 'Take his mina away from him and give it to the one who has ten minas.' 25 "'Sir,' they said, 'he already has ten!' 26 "He replied, 'I tell you that to everyone who has, more will be given, but as for the one who has nothing, even what they have will be taken away.'"

Each servant was given one mina (about three months' wages) and asked to steward that mina as he saw fit. One servant returns to share that he has turned his one mina into ten. The nobleman is ecstatic and rewards him control over ten cities. The second servant returns after turning his single mina into five. The nobleman again is thrilled and grants him control over five cities. Then we come to the last servant, who buried the one mina he was given and reports back happily that he's protected it. The nobleman is livid. He condemns the servant and is so furious that he takes his mina, gives it to the servant who had ten, and leaves him with nothing.

Our lives are supposed to bear fruit.

I think it's important to note that this story is not about money or financial gain. The money is a metaphor for the fruit our lives bear (or don't) as divinely-called creators and servants of Christ. In everything we do:

We are called to sow seeds.
We are called to act.
We are called to create.
We are called to win hearts for Jesus.

We are called to cling to our Creator in faith and live lives that fully express our God-given identities.

God's mission for our lives is written in the desires of our hearts. And those desires, if we are honest with ourselves, are radical, subversive — *revolutionary*. We have to overcome the fear, press through the over-analysis and the apathy, and choose the incredible lives we were designed to live.

In the renowned poem he penned in 1920, Robert Frost eloquently reminisces on how defining life's seemingly innocent choices can be:

THE ROAD NOT TAKEN

Two roads diverged in a yellow wood,
And sorry I could not travel both
And be one traveler, long I stood
And looked down the one as far as I could
to where it bent in the undergrowth;

Then took the other, as just as fair,
And having perhaps the better claim,
Because it was grassy and wanted wear;
Though as for that the passing there
Had worn them really about the same,

And both that morning equally lay
In leaves no step had trodden black.
Oh, I kept the first for another day!
Yet knowing how way leads on to way,
I doubted if I should ever come back.

I shall be telling this with a sigh
Somewhere ages and ages hence:
Two roads diverged in a wood, and I —
I took the one less traveled by,
And that has made all the difference.

When reading Frost's words, my heart can't help but be drawn to the passage in Matthew 7:13-14 when Jesus tells us the path is narrow and few will enter the kingdom. And in the weight of Jesus' words, my heart is breaking. It's in the separation that exists between where I've been, where I am today, and where I'm supposed to be, that I'm realizing how much all those seemingly inconsequential decisions mattered.

I know God has a way of making up for lost time, but it's hard not to morn for all of the opportunity I've wasted.

Thinking of myself and all of the people who don't choose the narrow road nearly enough, I can't help but wonder:

Why is the path that makes all the difference always the one less chosen?

I think it comes down to one simple truth: the narrow road is *not* easy. Our desires do not lead us down the road of least resistance. On the contrary, as any creator, artist, entrepreneur, or person who's found fulfillment in their life will tell you, the pursuit of our desires demands everything we have and more. It demands everything we have because choosing the path God has written on our hearts, means choosing to submit the entirety of our lives as clay to the potter, Himself — giving Him the to freedom to mold, shape, and refine us into the people He's always intended us to be. It's in this surrender that we allow God to breathe inspiration into our hearts and fulfill His desire to impact the world through our creative power.

It is in this communion with our Creator and the identity He's given us that we are able to truly become His hands and feet.

Being the hands and feet of God is a profound image. But as beautiful as the image is, this journey into the depths of our souls, into all of our possibility, that becoming a vessel requires, is anything but easy. This process of transformation, of release, is painful, devastating, beyond anything we can ever imagine — but the good news is that

God's love for us and His purpose for us is infinitely bigger than the struggle. God breaks us open because He desires to fundamentally restore us — at the very core of our being. And it is in the ashes of who we used to be, in the darkest moment of our fall, that our hearts are finally in a place to understand:

God is willing to shatter us *because* He's in love with us.

And the truth is, He shatters us because it's the only way He can save us. It is only when everything we've become has been stripped down to the foundation, to Ground Zero, that it's possible for our hearts to know who we truly are, how deep God's love is for us, and the incredible life for which He's preparing us.

I have a note card on my bedroom dresser. It's tucked into the corner of a framed photo of my best friend, Dusty, and me. On it I have a sentence dated March 20, 2011:

> *Unhappiness is nothing more than the result of our own rejection of the good and true and beautiful life that God has for us.*

I see the note every morning as I'm starting my day and it serves as constant reminder of the choice we are all presented with every breath we are given: *Are we willing to completely surrender everything we've become to discover everything God desires us to be?*

Unhappiness is nothing more than our soul's way of waking us up to the reality that we are living a life outside God's will for our lives. The agony is our heart's way of telling us that we have become a reservoir of the work God is trying to do in us and through us. God's road is indeed difficult, but peace comes when we discover just how much endurance can be found in Him and how much resolution can be found in letting go.

When we're able to trust the goodness of the orchestrator it becomes so much easier to separate the purpose from the pain.

Unhappiness is a victim mentality. The result of refusing to accept the truth that we have brought it on ourselves. We love to blame God for the lives and world we've created, for not experiencing the incredible life we've rejected, but it's our fault.

Every moment is a choice.

I don't have any stats to prove this, but I would venture to say the vast majority of people who reject the idea of God and Jesus do so on this argument: "How could a loving God allow so much pain in the world?"

It's a valid question, but it makes me want to ask some questions of my own:

Could it be that overwhelming pain exists in the world because humanity has overwhelmingly rejected God?

Is it possible that the pain only seems overwhelming because we have an overwhelmingly short-sided view of eternity?[1]

I think it's both.

We love to blame God almost as much as we love to proclaim our innocence and independence from Him.

Yes, God is able to work through all circumstances for good, but we are blinded by arrogance in rejecting the reality that we have blood on our hands. We have a short-sided view of life on this planet. It takes a humble heart to fully grasp the truth that our lives are nothing more than specks in the infinite context God enjoys. We are but dust of dust of dust, remember? Temporal pain and death are only negatives in our eyes because we as humans only understand one side of the coin. I bet if we had a full, eternal view, our sentiments might be a bit different. The truth is, we are ignorant, arrogant, selfish, and guilty. We are responsible for the lives we lead, whether we choose to give God an intimate role in it or not.

For better or for worse, with freedom comes responsibility.

Just as inaction always leads to failure, a Godless life will always result in a life of internal and eternal conflict. It is impossible to live the life we were designed to live apart from God because our Creator is wired into the very essence of our beings. We are all creators, created in His image. Our Creator dwells in us. Which means a denial of Him is, fundamentally, a denial of ourselves. In a deep and mysterious way, at some atomic level, us and our Creator are one in the same. If we really want to know the heart of God, we must give Him a chance to show us. Then, and only then, can we hold Him responsible. The ironic reality in all of this is that most of the people I know who have completely surrendered their lives to Jesus are evermore proclaiming His glory and thankfulness for His provision.

They are never disappointed.

Which is in extreme contrast to most of the people I know who've rejected God and seem to live lives full of conflict, turmoil, and resentment. It's as if they are at odds with the universe, as if Someone is out to get them. It's almost as if this Someone is so in love with them that He's doing whatever it takes to try and get their attention.

We are so stubborn and blind at times. It's as if our hearts become so hardened that our only hope of salvation lies in the hands of Someone who loves us enough to completely break us.

Funny how that works.

Even the ancient poet Rumi finds it ironic:

> *It's amazing, and funny, that you have to be pulled away*
> *from being tortured, pulled out*
> *into this Spring garden,*
> *but that's the way it is.*
> *Almost everyone must be bound and dragged here.*
> *Only a few come on their own.*
> *...*
> *There are two types on the path. Those who come*
> *against their will, the blindly religious people, and those*
> *who obey out of love. The former have ulterior motives.*[2]

As I've said, unlike humans, God loves simplicity. His call for our lives is simple: *Choose life.*

That's it.

Choose the life He is offering us, the life Jesus gave Himself for, in all it's beauty, eloquence, agony, and pain. Choose the path less traveled because the eternal stakes are higher than we can ever hope to fathom this side of Heaven. Choose the narrow road because any other will wither our souls. Choose life, choose God, choose Jesus, and choose to love the world the way He loves us. Love and give recklessly. Die to yourself, and I promise you will find life.[3]

I say all this because I've spent time on both roads. Each has broken me to my core, but only one ends in redemption and the full realization of the life we were made for. I am ignorant, arrogant, selfish, and guilty, and yet despite it all, God loved me so much that He chased me down — and continues to pursue me every day.

To be quite honest, God doesn't just chase us down. He hunts us down and tackles us. In the desperation of the moment, God tackles us like we're about to be hit by a bus. In the aftermath of the collision, we often find ourselves face down on the asphalt.

Bleeding.
Bruised.
Broken.

But alive.

Acts of heroism are not always pleasant, but they are always beautiful. And despite the beauty of God's ever-present heroism in our lives, He must constantly chase us because we constantly forget Him. We incessantly drift, sway, and wander.[4]

The narrow road is every bit as narrow as it sounds, but, oh, is the struggle to endure the journey worth it. Just like the note card on my dresser says, we must choose life. We must choose the narrow road.

Every moment of every day.

And believe me when I tell you, doing so will make all the difference.

EPILOGUE
THE BUTTERFLY EFFECT

"It has been said that something as small as the flutter of a butterfly's wing can ultimately cause a typhoon halfway around the world."

—*Chaos Theory*

A PARTING THOUGHT

MINE ALONE

Blinds left open,
In hopes that anything,
Might shine through.
The beams of a full moon.

But the moon remains stoic,
Content to let my heart wane.

Eyelashes are,
Nothing more than prison bars.
For eyes and a heart,
That seek but never find.

The pale light beckons for revelation,
But tonight the angels hold their tongues.
Their wings carry me no more,
The next step is entirely my own.

Hand in hand we've journeyed,
But the line, the unity, dissolves.
On my own, I now must stand.

The entire universe holds its breath,
In anticipation of what is about to come.
A day written in fire by the stars.

It is in this moment I now stand.
Guided by the firm hand of destiny.
Yet it is still mine to seize or deny.

Heaven drowns in tears at the thought.
The heart of God tears in our forsakenness.

The veil eclipses our bearings,
But in the darkness we are called to move.
Led by whispers of the saints,
Their words fall on our hearts like summer rain,
Yet burn with the fire of a thousand suns.

Lost in faith, we are rescued by love,
And at last we discover sanctuary.

But it is on my heart, on this breath,
The entire universe has pinned its axis.
Piercing my soul, the call resounds,
Wavering under its weight,
Recoiling, I do not fall.

For it is a destiny,
I have been chosen to receive,
One I now choose,
One that is entirely mine, alone.

Yet this moon-lit torch,
I do not carry for myself but for creation.

The universe suffocates in expectation,
Beckoned into the moonlight, I take the step.
And the universe thunders,
As the stars unite in exhale,
And tears of joy roll from the eyes of Heaven.

It is in our free will that God allows us to forsake not only Himself, but His calling for our lives. But it is also in our free will that God gives us the incredible opportunity to choose, and take ownership of, our divine purpose. I think each one of us inevitably reaches a critical moment, a crossroads, at some point in our lives where we must either choose, or walk away from, our calling. And in those moments, I believe all of Heaven sits in captive attention. The weight of the moment is incredible and the implications are incomprehensible no matter who you are, because each and every decision we make as individuals drastically changes the trajectory of the entire universe.

Whether we choose to believe it or not, our lives, our decisions, are infinitely transcendent. The butterfly effect is more real than we think. All of creation hinges on each and every person's choice to own or deny who they are and the purpose they have been called and created to fulfill.

What's more interesting, though, is that this choice really isn't about us, it's about everyone else. As it is for all of creation's benefit and joy that we must choose to pursue and fulfill our divine purpose.[1] Embracing the reality that our purpose often lies on the most difficult of paths, we must not seek to find joy in ourselves, but from the joy our purpose elicits in others.

We are lanterns — mirrors. We are designed to derive everything we are from outside ourselves — from God. Joy is no different. No matter how hard we try, we will never find happiness inside ourselves because that's not where it comes from. When we create joy in others through who we are, the world, the mosaic of humanity through which God reveals Himself, will reflect that joy back upon us.

Our lives and our worlds are reflections of who we are, of what we invest into them. We are defined by our generosity, by our service — by our sacrifice.

It's quite simple really, if you want to be fulfilled, fulfill the world. It is in the eyes of those we serve, in the hearts of those we inspire, that we catch the most vivid glimpse of who we are.

THE END

END NOTES

ONE **ANATOMY OF A SPARK**

1. Mark 8:35 — "For whoever wants to save his life will lose it, but whoever loses his life for me and for the gospel will save it."

2. James 4:14 — "Why, you do not even know what will happen tomorrow. What is your life? You are a mist that appears for a little while and then vanishes."

3. Psalms 103:14 — "For he know how we are formed, he remembers that we are dust."

4. Matthew 5:14-16 — "'You are the light of the world. A city on a hill cannot be hidden. Neither do people light a lamp and put it under a bowl. Instead they put it on its stand, and it gives light to everyone in the house. In the same way, let your light shine before men, that they may see your good deeds and praise your father in heaven.'"

5. For more on this, read *Broken Open* by Elizabeth Lesser. It's amazing.

6. Acts 1:8 — "But you will receive power when the Holy Spirit comes on you; and you will be my witnesses in Jerusalem, and in all Judea and Samaria, and to the ends of the earth."

TWO **CREATIVITY**

1. Ken Robinson gave a phenomenal TED Talk on this topic. You can watch it here:

http://www.ted.com/talks/ken_robinson_says_schools_ kill_creativity.html

2. For more on this, read *I Was Blind But Now I See* by James Altucher. It's one of my favorite books.

3. Rob Bell's book *Jesus Wants to Save Christians* is a great read if your interested in unpacking the book of Exodus.

4. There's a great article on the topic of the quarter-life crisis here:

   http://thedistrictweekly.com/2009/print/features/ quarterlife-crisis-coping/

5. *Love Wins* by Rob Bell (pg. 59)

6. Revelation 3:16 — "So, because you are lukewarm — neither hot nor cold — I am about to spit you out of my mouth."

7. For more on this, I highly recommend reading *The Slight Edge* by Jeff Olsen.

8. For more on this, I highly recommend reading *The Tipping Point* by Malcolm Gladwell.

9. Matthew 7:13-14 — "Enter through the narrow gate. For wide is the gate and broad is the road that leads to destruction, and many enter through it. But small is the gate and narrow is the road that leads to life, and only a few find it."

10. For more on this, read *The Screwtape Letters* by C.S. Lewis (pg. 39).

11. Here's the link to the video of Steve Jobs' famous speech:

http://www.youtube.com/watch?v=Hd_ptbiPoXM

12. Here's the link to the New York Times article about the study:

http://www.nytimes.com/2011/10/01/opinion/you-love-your-iphone-literally.html?_r=0

13. The song is called "Breathe (2am)."

14. Here's the link to the original tweet:

http://twitter.com/#!/louiegiglio/status/52935596565479424

15. The song was "Dare To Believe" by Boyce Avenue

16. Matthew 7:7 — "Ask and it will be given to you; seek and you will find; knock and the door will be opened for you."

THREE **FREEDOM**

1. I couldn't seem to find the original interview I watched, but here's a link to a talk Jack Dorsey gave at Stanford where he addresses the same idea:

http://youtu.be/fsOR-UvZ-hQ

Also, here's the written quote from the interview I couldn't find:

"I've often spoken to the editorial nature of what I think my job is, I think I'm just an editor, and I think every CEO is an editor. I think every leader in any company is an editor. Taking all of these ideas and editing them down to one cohesive story, and in my case my job is to edit the team, so we have a great team that can produce the great work and that means bringing people on and in some cases having to let people go. That means editing the support for the company, which means having money in the bank, or making money, and that means editing what the vision and the communication of the company is, so that's internal and external, what we're saying internally and what we're saying to the world – that's my job. And that's what every person in this company is also doing. We have all these inputs, we have all these places that we could go – all these things that we could do – but we need to present one cohesive story to the world."

2.   For more on this, read *Re-Work* by Jason Fried and David Heinemeier Hansson. It's one of the best books on business I've ever read.

3.   For more on this, read 80/20 by Richard Koch.

4.   According to research done by Nielson:

http://www.nydailynews.com/entertainment/tv-movies/americans-spend-34-hours-week-watching-tv-nielsen-numbers-article-1.1162285#ixzz272GtHRF5

5.   2 Corinthians 12:7-10 — "To keep me from becoming conceited because of these surpassingly great revelations, there was given me a thorn in my flesh, a messenger of Satan, to torment me. Three times I pleaded with the Lord to take it away from me. But he said to me, 'My grace is sufficient for you, for my power is made perfect in weakness.' Therefore I will boast all the more gladly about my weaknesses, so that Christ's power may rest on me. That is why for Christ's sake, I delight in weaknesses, in difficulties. For when I am weak, then I am strong."

6. Luke 17:33 — "Whoever tries to keep his life will lose it, and whoever loses his live will preserve it."

7. Just think, these paragraphs would have never existed had I decided an hour ago to not open my laptop. Does what I've written above have a purpose? I don't know. If I'm fully trusting in God's leadership, I don't have to worry about that. The purpose is in His hands. I'm merely the scribe. Either way, making the choice to respond to inspiration is always a win in my book.

8. Here's the link to the Steve Jobs interview video:

   http://www.youtube.com/watch?v=KuNQgln6TL0&feature=share

FOUR **ALL THINGS NEW**

1. I read three books that broke everything wide open: *Pagan Christianity* by George Barna and Frank Viola, *Revolution* by George Barna, and *Reimagining Church* by Frank Viola. They struck at the core of my heart's struggle and for the first time in my life, I realized I wasn't alone. The groaning in my soul was in fact a valid longing for the life God truly desired for me.

2. My translation analysis of the word *ekklesia* is based on the information provided by:

Blue Letter Bible. "Dictionary and Word Search for ekklesia (Strong's 1577)". Blue Letter Bible. 1996-2012. 8 Nov 2012. < http://www.blueletterbible.org/lang/lexicon/lexicon.cfm?strongs=G1577 >

3. For more on this, read *End of Religion* by Bruxy Cavey

4. Matthew 17:9 — "As they were coming down the mountain, Jesus instructed them, 'Don't tell anyone what you have seen, until the Son of Man has been raised from the dead.'"

5. If you didn't catch the reference, this video will get you up to speed:

   http://www.youtube.com/watch?v=EbVKWCpNFhY

6. From the book *Pagan Christianity* by George Barna and Frank Viola (pg. 176).

7. Acts 4:34-35 — "There were no needy persons among them. For from time to time those who owned lands or houses sold them, brought the money from the sales and put it at the apostles' feet, and it was distributed to anyone as he had need."

8. Here are few verses commonly quoted to validate Biblical support for paid pastors:

   Deuteronomy 25:4 — "Do not muzzle an ox while it is treading out the grain."

   1 Timothy 5:17-18 — "The elders who direct the affairs of the church well are worthy of double honor, especially those whose work is preaching and teaching. For the Scripture says, 'Do not muzzle the ox while it is treading

out the grain,' and 'The worker deserves his wages.'"

1 Corinthians 9:13-14 — "Don't you know that those who work in the temple get their food from the temple, and those who serve at the altar? In the same way, the Lord has commanded that those who preach the gospel should receive their living from the gospel."

1 Corinthians 9:15-18 is seldom included when verses 13-14 are referenced, but it's quite telling — "But I have not used any of these rights. And I am not writing this in the hope that you will do such things for me. I would rather die than have anyone deprive me of this boast. Yet when I preach the gospel, I cannot boast, for I am compelled to preach. Woe to me if I do not preach the gospel! If I preach voluntarily, I have a reward; if not voluntarily, I am simply discharging the trust committed to me. What then is my reward? Just this: that in preaching the gospel I may offer it free of charge, and so not make use of my rights in preaching it."

9. Acts 1:8 — "But you will receive power when the Holy Spirit comes on you; and you will be my witnesses in Jerusalem, and in all Judea and Samaria, and to the ends of the earth."

10. From the book *Revolution* by George Barna, Kindle location 435.

11. Matthew 7:7 — "Ask and it will be given to you; seek and you will find; knock and the door will be opened for you."

12. Matthew 8:10 — "When Jesus heard this, he was astonished and said to those following him, 'I tell you the truth, I have not found anyone in Israel with such great faith.'"

13. To clarify, I believe preaching is much different than teaching. I believe teaching is discipling and impossible to do from the pulpit.

14. Here's the link to the Donald Miller article:

http://donmilleris.com/2011/12/30/a-parable-about-the-church/

15. Matthew 7:7 — "Ask and it will be given to you; seek and you will find; knock and the door will be opened for you."

16. Acts 1:8 — "But you will receive power when the Holy Spirit comes on you; and you will be my witnesses in Jerusalem, and in all Judea and Samaria, and to the ends of the earth."

17. Matthew 11:30 — "For my yoke is easy and my burden is light."

18. Luke 10:27 — "He answered: 'Love the Lord your God with all your heart and with all your soul and with all your strength and with all your mind,' and, 'Love your neighbor as yourself.'"

19. Mark 12:28-31 — "'...Of all the commandments, which is the most important?' 'For the most important one,' answered Jesus, 'is this: 'Hear, O Israel, the Lord our God, the Lord is one. Love the Lord your God with all your heart and with all your soul and with all your mind and with all your strength.' The second is this: 'Love your neighbor as yourself.' There is no commandment greater than these.'"

20. Acts 1:8 — "But you will receive power when the Holy Spirit comes on you; and you will be my witnesses in

Jerusalem, and in all Judea and Samaria, and to the ends of the earth."

21. Genesis 3:19 — "By the sweat of your brow you will eat your food until you return to the ground, since from it you were taken; for dust you are and to dust you will return."

22. For more on this, read George Barna's book *Revolutionary*.

23. For more on this, please read *Epic* by John Eldredge. It's my favorite book on the Gospel. And the best part about it is you can read the whole thing in a couple of hours.

24. John 4:14 — "'...but whoever drinks the water I give him will never thirst. Indeed, the water I give him will become in him a spring of water welling up to eternal life.'"

25. Donald Miller wrote a great article about how we've become a church of academics:

    http://www.churchleaders.com/pastors/pastor-articles/158269-should-the-church-be-led-by-scholars-and-teachers.html?p=1

26. Revelation 21:5 — "He who was seated on the throne said, 'I am making everything new!' Then he said, 'Write this down, for these words are trustworthy and true.'"

FIVE **CHOOSE LIFE**

1. Isaiah 55:8 — "For my thoughts are not your thoughts, neither are your ways my ways, declares the Lord."

2. *The Essential Rumi* by Coleman Barks (pg. 175)

3. Matthew 10:39 — "Whoever finds his life will lose it, and whoever loses his life for my sake will find it."

4. If you have the time, read through Exodus to learn more about our forgetful nature. Rob Bell's book *God Wants to Save Christians* gives a great walk through Exodus as well.

EPILOGUE **THE BUTTERFLY EFFECT**

1. Galatians 5:13 — "You, my brothers, were called to be free. But do not use your freedom to indulge the sinful nature; rather, serve one another in love."

ACKNOWLEDGMENTS

My deepest thanks go out to the following people:

Drew Bodine and Bryan Boyd, for rescuing me in the Las Vegas desert.

Wes Guidera, for teaching me Photoshop.

Tim Fong, for journeying with me to find an alternative.

Jeff Remillard, for always picking up the phone.

My sister, Katelyn, for always being there, even when you're 5,000 miles away.

My parents, Greg and Sheila, for giving me the keys to the world — and for welcoming me home with open arms when the world won.

My wife, Jessica, for giving my restless heart the freedom to dream, create, fail, and dream again.

Gino Ivaldi and Terry Love, for letting me wash golf carts. For that opportunity, I am more indebted than you'll ever know.

Daniel Cordova, for that conversation at Starbucks.

Robb Moore, Ilan Kopecky and Todd Janzen, for giving me the chance to create for a living.

———

Mr. Bishop, for teaching me how to write and proving that English class could be gut-wrenchingly funny.

Ken Raskin, for being a friend, mentor, supporter, and spiritual leader, for all the dinners, oh, and for letting me marry your daughter!

Veronica Raskin, for all the spiritual council and conversations about my searching heart.

My uncle Bradley Lane Wright, for showing me at an early age what a true man of God looks like. Rest in Peace.

My grandfather Robert Leroy Wright, for teaching me the value of craftsmanship and for giving me the love of golf. Rest in Peace.

Ricardo Flores, for investing the time to help guide me through so many of my spiritual questions and struggles.

And last, but certainly not the least, Emily Watson, for pouring your heart and talent into editing the early manuscript. Thank you for making this engineer and designer look like he knows what he's doing.

———

ABOUT THE AUTHOR

Travis Wright lives with his wife, Jessica, in San Francisco, California, where he's the founder of Mirror, a creative studio that specializes in identity and product design for all available platforms from mobile to web. Previously, he founded SWL (Speak with Love), a philanthropic organization which used music and fashion as mediums to combat child hunger and sex trafficking. In his free time, you will find him reading, on the golf course, playing music, cooking up a world-class stir fry, or mucking around the house with his two crazy cats, Miko and Suki.

If you'd like to connect with Travis, you can find him online at:

Twitter: @travisewright
Email: spark@traviswright.org
Web: www.traviswright.org

www.ingramcontent.com/pod-product-compliance
Lightning Source LLC
LaVergne TN
LVHW051401080426
835508LV00022B/2919